MORNING RADIO:

A Guide To Developing On-Air Superstars

By:
Tracy Johnson
&
Alan Burns

ISBN 1-880846-88-8

TABLE OF CONTENTS

Section 2:
Three Steps To A Successful Show

Chapter 7:
Preparation

Chapter 8:
Concentration

Chapter 9:
Moderation

Section 3:
Comedy

Chapter 10:
Making It Funny

Chapter 11:
Types of Comedy

Section 4:
Evaluating The Show

Section 5:
Other Aspects

Section 6:

Hiring A Show

Section 7:

Musings

CREDITS & ACKNOWLEDGEMENTS

The Talent Tips followed by an * are from _Why Climb the Corporate Ladder When You Can Take the Elevator?_ by John M. Capozzi

Many of the ideas and principles were inspired from the work of one of America's best talent coaches, Randy Lane. Reach Randy at Randy@RandyLaneCo.com. Visit his web site at www.radiotalentcoach.com.

Also, thanks to Dan O'Day, who offers a variety of products and services to the radio industry at www.danoday.com. You can email Dan at danoday@danoday.com.

The authors would like to thank some of the people from whom we've learned, borrowed, or stolen ideas and information, and who have advanced the art and science of personality radio.

The list includes, in no particular order:

John Gehron	Larry Lujack	Jon Coleman
Dave Robbins	Guy Zapoleon	Dave McNamee
Steve Reynolds	Rick Dees	Robert Murphy
Kidd Kraddick	Jeff & Jer	Tommy Sablan
Randy Lane	Rick Cummings	Dan O'Day
Jeff Johnson	Dave Shakes	Steve Kingston
Don Anthony	Morning Mouth	Talentmasters
Network 40	Radio & Records	Hitmakers
Mike Kinosian	Tony Novia	Ries & Trout
ESP/Australia		

INTRODUCTION

Finding great air personalities that make a difference is more difficult — and more important — than ever before. The talent pool is shrinking, syndication is replacing local talent, and consolidation continues to change the nature of the radio industry.

Increasingly, it is apparent that air talent that truly makes an impact is not born, but created. The successful ones command huge salaries. But even if a station makes the financial commitment, there's no guarantee you'll get a show that is able to adapt the presentation to the market and the station, and ultimately pay off.

If you have time, growing your own show is an option. If you have more money than time, you can get there faster by luring the big morning show across the street. If you don't have time or money, you might be in trouble.

So what's a PD or GM to do? Syndication? Possibly, but national shows can't establish a personal, emotional bond with your listeners the way a local one can. Plus, the good ones aren't a cheap solution.

Syndicated shows are usually well established, consistent, and you know what you're going to get. After all, there is a track record in other markets. But, you lose the local aspect, and give up any hope of control or tailoring the show to your station.

Maybe the best solution is to grow your own personalities. It's a challenge to develop a great radio show. It's like planting a garden. It starts with planting a seed, developing a vision for the station and the show. With the proper care, adding resources, support, and marketing, your plants begin to grow. Then, through hard work and if you maintain reasonable, achievable and realistic goals, a beautiful harvest takes place, as you realize the cornerstone of a great radio station.

There are no immediate answers in most markets today.

Developing air talent is not easy. It takes patience! It takes an intense commitment and belief in the talent. And most of all, it takes time. Dominant, market-leading personalities won't just happen overnight. They are created, molded, and developed over time.

When growing a show with the hope of being more than just another "DJ," set your sites high. DJs are disposable. They're a dime a dozen. But celebrities have equity. They become larger than life. They help take a radio station to another "level" and help "bullet-proof" your radio station. By striving to develop *celebrities*, not just air personalities, the challenge becomes clearer, and petty distractions can be avoided. Becoming a celebrity takes time, talent, dedication, and an unending devotion to success.

Then, when you get one that works, cherish them. Treat them like the valuable property they are. That's when the real work begins. The proper care and feeding of big-time talent is an even bigger challenge. How can you manage and direct these sensitive, creative, and highly popular personalities? How can you motivate them to continue to grow? How can they be challenged to reach the next level? How can you critique without crushing that fragile ego? How do you help them stay focused? How can you establish a trust based on mutual respect?

Today's most successful air personalities are unique, individual talents. Their shows are as dissimilar as their markets. But almost every great personality has something in common. Scott Shannon, Rick Dees, Jeff & Jer, and Kidd Kraddick all have unique characteristics that separate them from the rest. It's a desire to succeed and be the best at what they do. Their dedication to the art drives them more than big salaries, ratings success, or the envy of the industry.

In our careers, we've worked with some of the best personalities in the business. We've built new shows from scratch, assembling dissimilar talent from various sources to challenge the market leader. We've tried fresh, new approaches, including an all female morning show, and modified tried and true recipes for success. Tracy has recruited Jeff & Jer to cross the street (twice) and challenged them to take their show to the next level. He helped recreate the show to be more relevant to an entirely new demographic.

The information in these pages reflects our personal beliefs and experiences, which have been influenced by years of working with great talent, programmers, and managers. The art of developing morning shows is cultivated through paying attention to audience feedback from focus groups, perceptual studies and ultimately, Arbitron ratings. The content here is a direct result of working with, for, and against some of the best in the business. A partial list of the most valuable contributors can be found in the back of the book. In fact, some of the content is a direct result of articles and ideas generated by them.

Through all of our successes and failures, every experience brings a lesson. But if there's one theme that keeps repeating, it's the essential thing about personalities: there is no secret "formula" that assures success. Developing personalities that define stationality is one of the most exciting and rewarding experiences in the business. With proper positioning, promotion, and presentation, personalities will become celebrities and your station will shine.

A couple of things about this book: there are many references to "morning shows." That's where great stations start, and it's generally accepted that morning drive is the most significant time slot. But that's not where it ends. The principles and information in this book apply to all talent.

Secondly, this work is directed to Program Directors and air personalities with the intention of helping develop talent. Take the principles, apply them, and work together to form a partnership that will make your station a dominant force.

The information in these pages reflects our personal beliefs and experiences, which have been influenced by some of the great talent and talent coaches in the world. Those who understand the process of creating a great morning show, and put into practice the art of making magic on the radio, are shining examples to all of us. They have helped form the philosophies and ideas in this book.

If you're an air talent, we hope it helps you become the next Rick Dees. If you're a PD, we hope it helps you develop the next Brandmeier!

SECTION

1

IT ALL STARTS IN THE MORNING

How important is a high profile morning show? Ask anybody who doesn't have one. It's vital. In most situations, a station without a strong morning show won't reach its potential. Go ahead—name a station that is a market leader, but doesn't have a high profile morning show. It may be successful, it may be competitive. But it's never going to be huge.

Think about the legendary radio stations in the 80s and 90s, and the morning shows that performed there.

> Z100/New York: Scott Shannon & the Morning Zoo
> KIIS/Los Angeles: Rick Dees
> Q105/Tampa: Q Morning Zoo
> KROQ/Los Angeles: Kevin & Bean
> KHKS/Dallas: Kidd Kraddick
> Q106 and Star 100.7/San Diego: Jeff & Jer
> WXKS/Boston: Matt Siegal

Great stations and great talent go hand in hand.

It makes no difference how strong your music is. Your competitors can clone that. Successful radio is all about stationality and establishing your station's unique mood in the mind of your listeners. The proper programming, marketing, and positioning of a station is a great subject, but that's another book. Once those elements are in place, the personality of the station takes on massive importance.

Everything starts with the morning show. Your station's mood, personality, and image are slave to the perception of your morning personalities. The old adage, "as goes the morning, so goes the rest of the day," is no myth. It's a basic truth of radio. Until the morning show is established, developing personalities in peripheral dayparts is ill advised. It just won't have the impact.

Without great air personalities, your station will sound like everyone else. The talent makes the difference. But morning shows are like fine sports cars. If one element is out of synch, the show won't work. And if the show doesn't work, neither does the station.

On the other hand, a poor morning show that *tries* to be great can prevent your station from ever getting off the ground. Just as a football team's chances of making the playoffs hinge on the success of its quarterback, a radio station revolves around the morning show. Smart programmers know this, and develop a "play book" to put the quarterback in a position to win. A great morning show can "bullet-proof" your station. It's your leverage to make every promotion bigger, every contest better. They're as important to a station as hands to a pianist.

A great morning show will take you to new heights, insulate you from the effects of a new competitor, and set the stage for the rest of the day.

HOW MUCH IS IT WORTH?

If the show is that important to your success, how much is it worth? First, throw out all the traditional rules. A great talent is worth their weight in gold. There are a few air personalities that are "franchise" players, but the great ones add millions of dollars a year to the bottom line. They protect the value of the station. Investing big bucks in a morning show is risky. Investing in the wrong show could waste millions of dollars. On the other hand, there are a lot of owners and managers that envy the successful risk takers. In today's market, you get what you pay for. It's typical to hear station management complain that there is no talent, no farm team, no great morning shows available. Then, they comment that they would never hire Howard Stern because they "can't sell it," or state "I'd never pay $xxx,xxx for an air talent." So, they hire a show they think they can sell, or one that costs less than the leaders, then wonder why they don't get the results they dream of.

You're not going to have a lot of numbers thrown at you in this book, but think about this: if you rank contemporary music stations in order based on the

> **Talent Tip:**
> The "intrinsic" value of a dominant morning show is difficult to measure, but is probably more valuable than any cost/return analysis on the daypart alone.

percentage of cume they convert to partisans, the top performing stations almost *always* have strong morning shows. Stations that lack a morning "star" might convert 25-30% of its cume to core listeners. Stations that have great personalities in the morning can convert up to 45% of their cume. That's a 50% difference! That's why a good morning show is so important. By increasing P1 conversion, you increase the entire station's TSL by half or more! As they say in the Ginsu Knife commercials...*Now how much would you pay*?

Performing in the morning show is a tough job. It's not 4-5 hours a day, five days a week, regardless of how it appears. Consider what air talent is asked to do. They get up in the middle of the night, do 4-5 hours of original material each DAY, and are often asked to create no controversy while fulfilling management's directive to turn the station into a winner. That's a tall order!

Yes, competing in morning drive can be expensive, and even then there are no guarantees that it will pay off. In the talent business, there are winners and losers, and little room for anything in between. So, if you're going to play in this arena, be prepared to pay the price of competing, relative to your market.

WHERE DO YOU FIND GREAT TALENT?

(And How Do You Know When You've Found It?)

"(Finding a morning show is) like making love to a woman. You may not always score, but when you do, it makes all the trying worthwhile."

> — *Chef (voice by Isaac Hayes, a morning personality himself) South Park, 1998*

F inding great talent is like searching for valuable coins with a metal detector. You turn up a lot of bottle caps and feel like you're wasting your time. But when (if) you find that rare nugget, it makes all the effort worthwhile.

First, be alert. Evaluate the entertainment value, not the radio show. Too many broadcasters get hung up on the "radio" part of our medium instead of the entertainment element. Some of the best radio personalities today are terrible DJs. In fact, they aren't DJs at all. Isaac Hayes and RuPaul knew little about radio, but bright programmers recognized the entertainment value and helped turn them into some of the most successful air talents of our time.

> **Talent Tip:**
> **It's usually easier to teach talented entertainers how to do good "radio" than it is to teach radio people how to be entertaining.**

Be alert to any possibility. Don't worry about formatics. Personalities don't have to give the time and temp, or be "tight and bright." They command attention and big dollars because they entertain and create attention. Look for those unique personalities that can add to your station's personality profile. You can figure out how to provide the service elements later.

Search for charisma, a talent that is more than just another voice on the radio. Step out of the box and listen for the entertainment potential of candidates. Don't listen to what they say. Listen to how they make you *feel*.

But how do you know the right type of personality to look for? Start your search with the attitude of "I don't know exactly what I'm looking for, but I'll know when I find it." This will help you listen with an open mind and stay clear of preconceived notions.

Finding Talent

Many broadcasters are finding talent in non-traditional areas. The key is to find interesting, entertaining people who are willing to learn how to make a dynamic personality work on the radio.

Instead of scouring competitors or smaller stations for talent, try local comedy clubs or theater groups. Is there a well-known celebrity or performer that lives in your area? How about a cab driver or bus driver? Have you met a waiter or waitress that is engaging and presents themselves well? You never know where you might find compelling personalities.

When an Alan Burns & Associates client needed new talent, an on-air "star search" turned up a medical technician who had a great voice, compelling personality, and intense desire to be on the radio. The woman went on to become the star of the show! This "non-radio" focus also paid off by producing a comedy writer who'd just moved to the market.

Also, don't overlook the possibility of using technological advances to your advantage. Your next high profile personality may be on the air in another market today, and not even have to relocate!

CHARACTER TRAITS OF WINNING SHOWS

Success on the air is more a function of consistent common sense than of creative genius. Most personalities make it too difficult.

So what are the key elements that make up a great show? There are as many types of personalities as there are personalities. But, there are common traits that many winning shows share. Here are some traits that are on the "shopping list" of many PDs:

- **They are not fake**. The best shows give the impression that listeners are eavesdropping on a conversation, and often participate in it. It is imperative that the players on the show genuinely like each other. It should be natural. You can't perform 240 shows a year, over 1,000 hours of material, and fake it successfully. The "real" personality will come through and the audience will discover the fake.

- **They are likeable.** Sarcasm and cynicism have a place on some shows, but rarely make up the core attributes. Even Letterman has seen audience erosion over the years. Most humor should be victimless, or targeted back on themselves. Don Rickles made a career out of a comedy act that generated laughs at the expense of others, but his routine was in short doses.

- **They are well balanced.** Consistency is their virtue. Listeners fatigue of a steady diet of the same material. Great shows provide diversity and creativity within the same personality. They present a variety of materiel consistent with their persona.

- **They are credible.** They stay true to the personality and positions represented. Winning shows know what the audience expects, and delivers. They never violate the audience's trust.

- **They are entertaining.** Not always funny, but usually fun. They spend hours in preparation. They sound spontaneous, but it's the result of endless hours of planning and brainstorming.

- **They are interesting.** Never boring. They do things to get attention. They brainstorm ways to come up with new angles to old bits that will create talk. They understand that this is show biz!

- **They are visible.** They meet listeners, shake hands. They pick events and appearances carefully for maximum impact. There's no room for laziness. Becoming a winning personality is like running for public office. You have to meet the constituents, the people casting their "votes." If you kiss enough babies and shake enough hands, you may win the election!

- **They are humble.** At promotions a talent may be a star and the center of attention. But on the air, they are a friend. Egos running out of control generally repel listeners. They understand the idea of being important by putting others in the spotlight.

- **They have a purpose.** They make it a mission to deliver for the audience. It's bigger than a paycheck or a ratings bonus. It's an inner drive and passion that makes it work.

Before you can identify your winning personality, you must understand *Your Station*! A director would never cast a movie before reading the script. How can you possibly cast your new personalities,

> **Talent Tip:**
> **Don't start looking for talent until you truly understand the station!**

unless you first know what the station is all about, and what your ultimate goals are? Howard Stern commands a huge audience, but the audience he attracts may be inconsistent with your audience's expectations. It may be great for the morning show, but devastating for the radio station. To make it work, the talent must have an appreciation and understanding of the station's goals, and management must help talent reach their career goals. Miscasting the show will make everyone miserable.

Finally, once you know the station, get to know your target audience. Understand their values, lifestyles, attitudes, and opinions. What is their point-of-view? What unique qualities about your station appeal to your audience? How do you fit into their lifestyle? More importantly, what do listeners remember about you? Once a clear view of what they are all about emerges, you can begin to define what the personalities should sound like.

What Is Stationality?

Usually when you think of the term "personality" you think of the character, disposition, or overall feeling that is portrayed by a person. But every station also has a personality. It is a sum total of all the elements of a station.

Everything contributes to the stationality: music, promotional announcements, the signature voice that is chosen, production elements, commercial load, commercial content, personalities, everything.

In the early 90s, one of the country's most respected CHR stations faced a problem that proved to be impossible to overcome. The well-known and highly popular morning show had evolved into a product that appealed mostly to men. Meanwhile, the station's music was (correctly) geared toward women.

Several program directors attacked the problem. They adjusted the music. Big cash contests were implemented. Production elements were changed. The morning show personalities had such an impact on the station's overall personality that all attempts to reconcile the images into a focused entity failed.

Eventually, the station was sold, the format changed, and the staff was replaced.

Programmers must select personalities as carefully as they choose the music. It all must add to the desired station personality. Stations with great elements do not become great stations because the elements are not synchronized to create a well-defined stationality. If the personality of the morning show doesn't coincide with the personality of the station, one or the other must change, or disaster awaits.

CHAPTER

2

THE PD/TALENT RELATIONSHIP

"It's what you learn after you know it all that counts"

> — *John Wooden,*
> *former UCLA Basketball Coach*

Successful stations always have successful talent. And market dominant talent always works on successful stations. The key relationship is the talent and the programmer.

A great program director has many diverse roles: leader, manager, mentor, judge, coach, therapist, counselor, cheerleader, and negotiator. They have to do it all. Some are able to do it well, others struggle with some of the roles. But all are important to talent.

Regardless of the many "hats" today's PD has to wear, the better the programmer understands the talent, the more equipped he or she will be to work with them.

To find, recruit, and manage a winning morning show, you have to understand their point of view, what makes them "tick." In general, morning shows don't understand, and in some cases don't agree with, the goals of the stations they are on. There's a huge communication gap. Until the talent, the producer, and the programmer all get "on the same page," you won't realize success. So, before the morning show utters its first words on a radio station, they must know and believe in the strategic and tactical goals of the station and how they fit into the plan.

Understand that talent is vulnerable. It would be hard to name another job where performance is under such heavy scrutiny, and not just by the boss. They get critiqued by the boss' wife, friends, clients, and sales people. Everything they do is under a microscope, and it affects them. It would hurt anybody, let alone these highly sensitive individuals!

Imagine what that must be like. What if every meeting you conduct, every memo you write, is under the same examination? Write that note with the wrong tone and you get criticized. Send the "wrong message" and there'll be a special interest group gathering in the lobby in protest, campaigning to have you fired. That's what it's like to be on the air, to lay your heart out every day.

Why is talent so insecure and wary? Think about it. They've been mistreated, lied to, used and been the scapegoat. Why should they trust the GM or PD? Talent is

Talent Tip:
An effective PD will be perceived as the talent's biggest fan!

usually the first to go if the station has to change format. They've been burned dozens of times in their career. It's part of the nature of this industry, and they've learned the only way to survive is by "looking out for #1." It's not right, but that's the way it is.

It's up to the programmer and manager to gain their respect and trust. The responsibility is on management to build a partnership and help them achieve their goals! To keep them performing at their best, you must make them feel secure. Management's success is so dependent on talent's success, why would you not treat them like the important assets they are? Yet, insecure PDs let their egos get in the way.

Talent Tip:
It takes five years of hard work to become an instant success.*

A morning radio show is like no other job. It's not 8 hours a day, 40 hours a week. The best talent prepares ALL the time. They're always thinking about the show, crafting real life experiences into interesting material to use on the air. It's a passion. Their hours are usually unlike any other. They are almost always tired, and few people understand what they go through. Most of the public and staff envy them because "they only work 3-4 hours a day," then blow out of the station and are unreachable. In reality, nothing could be further from the truth.

That's like saying Michael Jordan got $30 million a year just for playing a child's game three hours a day, three days a week, six months a year. NO! Michael's domination of the NBA was the result of a lifetime of preparation, and he never stopped training, preparing, evolving, changing. The public only saw the *result* of his hard work and the glory that went with it.

When approaching talent, PDs must be "on their side," making talent aware that they appreciate how much of themselves they give. Communicate with them and earn their respect. Show them that you understand your goals and theirs are inseparable.

Talent should be a priority for all managers. More than money, they work for recognition. They strive for recognition in the press, from fans, from trade publications, from peers, and especially from their *boss*.

In radio, there is no studio audience, and listeners may not react on the phones. In a way, they perform in a void. The PD must fill that void. A salesman might work harder in the relentless pursuit of commissions, even if he or she doesn't get their ego stroked occasionally. If their manager treats air talent the same way, the talent will start to worry they are about to be fired. Similarly, talent can let the phones give them unreliable feedback and distort a bad idea. The PD has to keep them on an even keel.

The PD — as their manager — is in a position to be their representative, their ambassador to greatness. A PD's goal is to use their abilities and celebrity status to protect the station from competitive attack. Likewise, a talent's goal should be to use the resources and support of the station to increase their celebrity status beyond anything they could achieve on their own.

After all, you're on the same team. The PD/Talent relationship is like that of a coach and athlete. There will be disagreements, and unavoidable conflicts, but if you have a strong relationship based on trust, communication, and mutual respect, it's easy to reconcile. You're family. You may not always LIKE each other, but you always LOVE one another, and heaven help the other guys who attack a family member!

With the amount of pressure on your talent, the PD is the one they relate to, the one that shelters them from the distractions and peripheral demands. The PD is the one who understands and appreciates them, the one that shields them from the sales department. They won't be successful without the backing and support from management. Their confidence comes from management. And they have to be FEARLESS on the air. They should never feel like they perform for the PD, or be fearful that the break they just did will bring on their boss' wrath. No matter what happens, the PD is the #1 fan!

Get To Know Your Talent!

(How Tracy learned a lesson the hard way)

One of the biggest mistakes in my programming career eventually led to a sequence of events that cost me my position.

I had just inherited the PD position at a top rated, but declining, CHR station with a market dominant morning show. My marching orders were to halt the ratings erosion, bring a more contemporary sound to the morning show, and prepare the station for the future.

Well, I had all the answers. My strategic and tactical plans were perfect, and we were going to make a difference! Changes were made with enthusiasm, flair, and conviction.

But I didn't enlist the talent as part of the solution. In fact, I didn't even consider that they had insight into the station and the market that might be helpful. I just pushed ahead.

Predictably, the morning show that I was going to "fix" behaved very badly, on and off the air. But instead of establishing a relationship and getting to know my highly sensitive personalities, I reacted by pulling further away from them.

We ended up with a station that had a great plan, but nobody to make it happen, because nobody *believed* in it. I learned one of the most valuable lessons of my programming career: It doesn't matter if you are *right* if everyone responsible for executing the plan lacks confidence.

In hindsight, it's obvious that I could have avoided the problem and probably salvaged a pretty good gig by slowing down, asking questions, and appealing to all of the talents' willingness to help make the station a winner.

EFFECTIVE MANAGEMENT STYLES FOR AIR TALENT

PDs have many styles, and some are more effective with highly talented performers than others. All talent is different and there are as many approaches as there are personalities.

But, depending on the level of ability, maturity, and development, the PD may exercise more or less control.

If you have new, inexperienced talent or personalities with limited ability, you'll want to control more of the show. For maximum impact, the PD will want to act as the **Director** of the show in most every area. This is an effective method of managing a new show or one that is struggling to find its place.

If the talent has a good feeling about where the show is positioned and where it needs to go, many PDs will find it effective to manage through **Persuasion**. This offers a moderate amount of direction and control through explanation and demonstration. It's a process that takes a little more time, and relies upon communication skills. You should use this approach in situations where you have talent with good ability, good attitudes, and a willingness to learn and respond.

If you're particularly fortunate, and have a talented show that is experienced, professional, and polished, you may be able to act as the show's **Counselor**. However, this can be disastrous unless you really know what you are doing. A PD that gives up direction and control of the show has a hard time getting it back, so proceed with caution.

Finally, if you have world class talent that is truly leading the station, the talent takes control of the show with your input and ideas. The PD's goal is to keep them aligned with the station's goals. Use only with senior talent and experienced personnel!

Bear Bryant

One of the greatest college football coaches of all time was Coach Paul "Bear" Bryant at the University of Alabama. The Bear would have made a great program director or talent coach because he was able to get the most out of his people. In fact, a rival coach once honored Bryant by commenting that "Bryant is one of the only coaches ever who can take his team and beat yours, or take your team and beat his."

Bryant had a very simple, straightforward policy that we can all learn from. He lived his life by this simple code:

> If everything goes great, **YOU** did it.
> If it goes moderately well, **WE** did it.
> If anything goes wrong, **I** did it.

His players were fearless, and would perform with the confidence that their coach would back them up, on and off the field, and Bryant was rewarded with a lifetime record that has been matched by few in history.

THE COACH/ATHLETE RELATIONSHIP

To have a successful show, the relationship must have the right tone. It takes a great deal of time, support, and tremendous dedication to make it work. It also takes a keen sense and understanding of where the talent is on the "development curve."

"Coaching" is one of the hottest buzzwords in management today. Proper coaching produces long-term benefits in the grooming of talent, especially morning shows. Coaching refers to continuous development of employees to help them perform their job better. It involves an assessment of development needs and training.

An air personality is like a great athlete. Put them in an arena where they can excel and stand back. You will marvel at what they can do on the field. Great talent make good PDs look like heroes. A PD's role is that of a coach, offering direction, support, encouragement, training, focus; and yes, critique, correction, and discipline are essential ingredients. Helping talent achieve the "next level" of performance requires intense dedication and patience.

A good coach knows how to get information from the "athlete" without making the person feel as if he or she is

> **Talent Tip:**
> **Don't mistake control for leadership.**

being interrogated. It involves listening, asking the right questions, and letting the other person respond. Paying attention to their thoughts, concerns, worries, and fears will give you signals of how to formulate a plan to influence behavior.

Proper coaching means being aware of what is happening "on the field" or, in the case of radio, inside the station. Identify internal problems and challenges so you can address these issues as they arise.

Finally, a good coach offers feedback with instruction. Feedback is vital to the performance of an athlete and talent. This applies to praise for a job well done and instruction to correct negative performance.

There is so much riding on the success of air talent. It's perhaps the most important responsibility in the PD job description. Great PDs understand that feedback is of primary importance. Like great coaches, great

PDs realize that talent is far more qualified to know *how* to perform. The PD has to put talent in the environment to be the best they can. The PD creates the playbook that takes advantage of his athlete's skills.

The PD also must help talent integrate into the station's strategy (offense). That means the PD must actually have a strategy. Do you know what it is? Does your staff know? As you develop strategies, design it around the offensive weapons you have on your team. It makes no sense to have a winning strategy but not the talent it takes to execute. And remember your "players" must communicate the message you want delivered.

THE IMPORTANCE OF FEEDBACK

Providing regular input should occupy a large part of every PD's day. When air personalities don't get constant feedback, they will do things to get attention. Usually bad things. Anything to get a reaction from you. It's not necessarily intentional, just a way of letting you know they need to hear from you!

When offering feedback, be consistent. Talent places enormous emphasis on comments made to them directly. What the PD likes and dislikes must be consistent, or the talent will become confused. A good rule of thumb is to offer only 1-2 criticisms per day. A long list of concerns about the show will crush a talent's ego. The daily show meeting is a perfect forum for this feedback, but a less formal conversation in the hall can have more impact.

All talent responds better when you emphasize strengths rather than criticizing weaknesses. They should always have a chance to respond to criticism. If they are expected to respond in the desired way, they have to understand and "buy into" the nature of the feedback. Everyone has to be on the "same page." If the feedback is one-way, you may get compliance but it won't be converted into action.

> *Talent Tip:*
> *Accentuate the positives. Talent will go out of their way to make you happy, if you tell them what it is you like!*

The best "coaches" give their talent a game plan to win, and are also great listeners. They show interest in arriving at decisions to improve the talent. They listen carefully to gauge the level of understanding of their talent. They try to motivate and stimulate their talent, not bully them into submission.

Feedback should never come because of listener complaints. Complaints are a healthy sign. You're getting reaction! Talent should never know about complaint calls, unless management is trying to clarify something that happened so they can respond to complaints. When talent hears about listeners calling in, they assume the PD agrees, and they start to worry or second-guess their performance.

Traits Of Great PD/ Talent "Teams"

Successful relationships are built around an understanding that successful radio is a two-way street. Like a marriage, air talent and management must respect the partnership, and work hard to nurture it. Here are some of the elements that help establish a winning relationship:

1. **Respect. Respect goes both ways.** Both parties must be committed to an honest, open relationship. Success is shared, and so is responsibility for falling short. Don't hold any grudges. Michael Jordan and Phil Jackson had this type of rapport, and the result was the greatest run of championships in NBA history.

2. **Agreed-Upon Expectations.** Talent and PDs must know what to expect from each other, and what will be considered acceptable. Only then can they identify when something is "off." Establish the ground rules up front and avoid problems later.

3. **Partnership.** Just like an actor and director work together to make motion picture magic, the PD and talent form a bond that is inseparable. The actor makes the movie sparkle, but the director defines the outcome. They win and lose together. There are individual roles, but common goals.

4. **Honesty.** Every day. There's no room for games, politics, or second-guessing. It only leads to fear and mistrust. Be clear, honest, straightforward, and direct in dealing with each other at all times.

5. Support. PDs are facilitators, not dictators. The great PDs help talent grow as individuals while building a winning team. Talent is enabled when they have the tools to succeed. The PD may not have all the answers, but must be willing to help the talent find the answers.

6. Interest. Great coaches are great listeners, and listening shows interest. Concentrate on strengths while strengthening weaknesses. This helps build trust.

7. Creativity. Study the creative process. There is always room to improve. The more you hang out together and get to know each other, the more you will appreciate and learn from each other. Push each other to be better. Think from a listener's perspective.

8. Critique. Criticism goes both ways. It's vital to allow talent to critique themselves first.

MAKE THEM FEEL LIKE STARS

One of the biggest challenges a programmer faces is developing personalities that will make the station stronger, and controlling the inevitable ego problems that result. Many PDs end up

> **Talent Tip:**
> **Develop confidence in your talent by letting them enjoy the celebrity status they crave.**

explaining to talent that "the station is the star." Telling that to an air talent is like telling a salesman they have to work for free! The motivation is destroyed!

Great air talent works in this business for notoriety. The challenge is to let them have their stardom, and work to take advantage of their celebrity. Talent will appreciate it, and as a result, feel more secure and confident. That leads to better performance. Confident talent is productive talent. Don't be afraid of their celebrity. Help them develop it. Use their desire to be famous to help you win!

> **Talent Tip:**
> **To paraphrase Tom Cruise's character in the hit movie Jerry McGuire, "Help talent help you." Enlist their knowledge and experience to assist you in programming the station. Make them feel that they are the station's "Assistant PD."**

At the same time, talent should never be allowed to think of the show as "theirs." It's the station's show, and it's the PD's responsibility to manage the talent to get the most out of them for the station. It's a partnership and it will dramatically influence the success or failure of the station.

To foster the partnership, talent should be involved in the radio station. They should be part of the programming process. They have valuable information. They have a different perspective than you do. They know what listeners say about the station. They're on the front lines. PDs should use their experience and expertise in programming the station. Talent should never find out second hand about any programming changes. They should be part of the decision!

When considering programming changes, take into account the talent on your team. Can they help you make it happen?

TOOLS & SUPPORT

Just as an actor can't be as effective without props and scenery, an air talent needs the tools to be effective. Relative to the payoffs that are involved, most of the tools are very inexpensive. It's like making sure an electrician has the best wire cutters available when you send him out to do his job.

Talent Tip:
Always make sure you have what you need before you begin.*

Some shows need more support than others. Dick Purtan recently had as many as *sixteen* people working on his show. You may not need, or be able to afford, that luxury. Some of you probably run your entire station with fewer employees. The example is for perspective. If your morning show needs some prep services, for example, it's really not unreasonable, difficult or expensive to provide.

Talent needs very little, really, to win. The great ones work hard, and much of that work isn't noticed. It happens outside the station. Talent has to be able to live the life of their listeners. A lot of time and emotional energy goes into tapping into those emotions. The least you can do is provide the elements to win.

COMMON MISTAKES A PD CAN MAKE WITH TALENT

To better understand the coach/player relationship and better support the air talent, here are some mistakes programmers and managers should avoid:

1. **Providing critical, negative feedback.** Most good talent is already very critical of themselves. They don't need to have their shortcomings hammered home. The best way to work with talent is to coax better performances through emphasis of their positive aspects. Encourage them to repeat those actions. You can't badger athletes into better performance! Talent is far more critical of their own performance than anyone else can be.

2. **Offering subjective feedback.** If you can't offer solid, objective reasons and support for your criticism, keep your mouth shut. Don't just say "that break was too long." Have a reason how and why it was too long. If the boss tells a worker he doesn't like the way he performs on the job, but doesn't explain why he feels that way, the supervisor loses credibility. Some talent have little respect for PDs because it's obvious they don't relate to the process of building a morning show.

3. **Providing generalized feedback.** Even if it's positive, vague praise raises more questions than it provides confidence. The talent will wonder what it is that you mean, exactly. It also can be dismissed as a patronizing stroke. Try telling a child, "Hey, you were really good today." It doesn't work. You have to be specific. Tell them exactly what they did well, and how what they did makes you happy. Let talent know how they contributed to a win, and you will get positive performance regularly.

4. Providing feedback that emphasizes mechanics over content.
Emphasizing formatics sends the message that details are more
important than entertainment. This leaves them feeling insignificant.
If your talent is going to make a difference at your station, it's
through what they do, not how they do it. Imagine an NFL coach
talking to John Elway about throwing off his back foot when the
Broncos are driving to a game-winning touchdown. Ridiculous!

5. Providing little feedback of any kind. Talent wants to know what is
going on. They want to know where they stand, and PDs owe that to
them. The head coach has to talk to his quarterback!

6. Suggesting they can improve by listening to other personalities.
You want your show for the talent they bring, not for their ability to
imitate other shows. However, listening critically to other shows can
be valuable if used properly. Learn from other shows, but never, ever
suggest they be like other talent. What would happen if Ken Griffey
Jr. changed his swing to be more like Mark McGwire?

**7. Issuing direct orders or strong suggestions on topics based on
your interests.** Talent is best when they feel passionately about
things. You can't force your ideas or standards on them. It'll be flat
and emotionless.

8. Playing games. Don't patronize them, or ask leading questions
designed to get them to do what you want. Be direct, up-front, and
honest. Let them know how much you need them. Like a boxer and
his trainer, you have to level with each other. If you want them to do
you a favor, ask them for a favor. Don't try to trick them.

9. Assuming that every complaint is valid or negative. Most
complaints and criticisms are not deserved. Talent doesn't need to
know about it. Deal with it. You're their shield. Protect them. Just
like a head coach will take the rap for losing the game by telling the
media he called the wrong play.

10. **Discussing any program or segment without a common vision for the show.** Without establishing common ground up front, it's impossible to gauge progress or set a standard for evaluating execution. What role do they play? What is expected? You can't criticize a point guard for not scoring points if he thinks his role is to run the court and set up his teammates.

11. **Discussing the show without understanding specific performance elements needed to make it work.** What makes something relatable to the audience? Who IS the audience? Have you done your homework? A coach doesn't talk to his quarterback about this week's game if he hasn't studied his competition and how to exploit their weaknesses.

12. **Providing suggestions for improvement based on assumptions of the talent's goals.** When a bit fails to hit home, first try to analyze what the intention was. Then, discuss how it fell short. Bridge the gap between the goal and the result. Don't try to change the idea. That's dealing with a symptom. Your job is to help solve the problem and treat the cause.

CHAPTER 3

THE RECIPE

Tell me, I forget.
Show me, I remember.
Involve me, I understand.

Like a house specialty prepared by a gourmet chef, the exact recipe for a successful show will vary from station to station. So how do you develop your own secret recipe of programming a great morning show that complements and eventually leads the station? What ingredients go into the mix that give something unique, that the competition just can't match? It's simple really:

1. Hire Great Talent

2. Make Them Understand What's Expected

3. Give Them Support and Direction

4. Let Them Be Creative

5. Then, Pay Them What They're Worth

You must work to avoid the petty differences that come between a staff and morning show. Never allow jealousy to get in the way of success. You're all on the same team!

As you put the show together, you must first understand what the morning show is all about through the only opinions that matter—your listeners.

Step 1: Hire Great Talent.

> **Talent Tip:**
> **When you pay peanuts,**
> **you get monkeys.***

Don't compromise. It may be impossible to find the "perfect" talent, but never settle for something secondary. Going into a new talent situation on a hope and a prayer with an attitude of "well, it *might* work" is almost always an entrée into failure. It's better to keep looking than it is to hire someone just to "get on with it."

Step 2: Make Them Understand What's Expected.

The communication process starts early in the relationship between PD and talent. Before signing off on the contract terms, everyone should be aware of what is being expected of the show. Is this show the "savior" of the station? Tell them. Is it to help take the station to the next level? Tell them. Is it to complement the excellent programming that already exists and not "get in the way" of the other elements? Tell them. Is it to take on the "most music in the morning" position and deliver service elements? Tell them. Management must know *why* they are hiring talent, and talent must know *what* management expects them to achieve.

Step 3: Give Them Support and Direction.

Never leave talent "hanging," hoping they are making you happy. Set up criteria to measure performance and direction on how to help achieve success. Make sure needed support staff and tools are available for the talent to deliver what you expect from them.

Step 4: Let Them Be Creative.

Help them help you! If the hiring process was executed properly, the personalities are capable of bringing dimension, personality, and sizzle to the station that you can never achieve without them. Don't tell them how to do their job, just help them do it better! Many managers hire a morning show, then over-manage, thereby suppressing the very characteristics that attracted them in the first place.

Step 5: Pay Them What They're Worth.

Don't be penny-wise and pound-foolish. It's much less expensive to take care of winning talent than to have to try and replace (or worse, *compete* with) the talent that helped the station become successful.

Find The "Right" Answer— Together!

The relationship between PD as "coach" and talent as "athlete" often breaks down over petty, egotistical issues. Both sides want to be "right."

But what is "right?" For every problem or question, there are at least 10 possible solutions. Of the possibilities, it's safe to assume that 20% are so "wrong" that no matter how well the plan is executed, it can't possibly work. 20% are so "right" that no matter how poorly it's executed, it won't fail. Then there are the 60% that, with the proper commitment, teamwork, and focus, *can* work.

Your goal should be to avoid the "absolutely wrong" answers, while finding the "absolutely right" answers.

But at all costs, agree on the solution that you will execute together and *make it work*.

Nobody has all the right answers all the time. If talent and coach commit to finding the right answer together, it *will* work.

GETTING IN SYNCH

After establishing the relationship, the PD must ensure that talent understands what's important to the station! Conduct a seminar on the demographic and psychographic makeup of the target audience. Let them sit in on focus groups to understand how listeners' perceptions are formed. Explain how and why the station is programmed and marketed the way it is. The PD and talent should spend at least an hour a day the week before the show's debut just taking them to "school."

By helping talent reach an understanding of company goals and their role in making the company a winner, they become partners in the process. Let them know how much you are counting on them for your success, how much they mean to

> **Talent Tip:**
> **Give talent a stake in the success of the station. Help them understand how the "team's" wins are in their best interest.**

your company. Spell it out to them up front. Make it specific. Show them how they will be more popular than ever as a result. BUT, stop short of telling them HOW to do it. They're the pros. Let them perform!

Your morning show really wants to make you happy, to earn the high salary they seek. Your job is to make them feel appreciated and give them the support they need to be successful.

THE MISSION STATEMENT

Most successful companies have a corporate mission statement of at least a few lines or paragraphs that capture the essence of what the business is all about, and how it plans to be successful. Mission statements help focus employees on what is and isn't important. It specifies company priorities and establishes standards by which to measure success.

> **Talent Tip:**
> **Many shows fail because nobody has defined to them what constitutes a "win."**

After agreeing on the psychographic makeup of the audience, it's a perfect time to construct a mission statement for the show. Like the company's statement, the show's mission statement sets a standard to evaluate the show's success without resorting to Arbitron. It's a document that settles arguments, helps evaluate performance, and breaks ties. A properly written (and committed to) statement will give you a foundation on which to build the entire show.

When constructing your mission statement, have everyone involved in the show (including the GM and even other personalities) create several lists. Be sure to include:

1. What do you want the audience to say about you one year from today?

2. What emotions do you want to stoke in your audience?

3. Fill in the blank from a listener's perspective....The morning show is JUST LIKE ME because _____.

4. What will the audience remember about the show, and about the individual performers?

5. What is "the line" of good taste that will never be crossed?

Then, take several hours outside the office and prioritize all the lists. Get everyone to agree on what is important to the show. Finally, combine all of the

> **Talent Tip:**
> **Develop a mission statement together that reflects the goals of the team and the individual.**

objectives in a definitive statement that acts as the source for evaluating all morning show elements.

Once you settle on the statement, the next step is to do everything possible to become intimately acquainted with the lifestyle, mood, attitude, and point-of-view of the audience. Live your life through the target's eyes. Share their concerns and fears about family, money, love, sex, relationships, careers...everything!

> **Talent Tip:**
> **A talent's mission statement must complement the station's mission statement. That means the station must actually have a mission statement.**

This is exhausting work. Great shows are constantly observing, reflecting, and associating with the target audience. Then, they figure out how to portray these values on the air. Great shows read what THEY read, watch what THEY watch. They don't have to be in the same demo, but must be in touch with the target.

A Failed Mission Statement

Several years ago, I had the brilliant idea to revolutionize the radio industry and shake up the market by creating an all-female morning show. After all, what could be more appropriate for a station targeting women than a show that reflects their lives and experiences?

For many reasons, the show was a miserable failure. The personalities were terrific, and the concept will work. My fatal mistake was not establishing a viable mission statement with the talent. As my frustration with the show increased, they became distant and bad things happened on the radio. I tried to work with them on changing their on-air approach, but they thought I was "out to get them." Why? We had not established specific standards of what would be the essence of the show. There was nothing to objectively measure their performance, and what started out as a positive relationship turned adversarial.

Our mission statement was vague, naïve, and useless. It was, essentially:

"The show will be by women, for women, consistent with the demographic goals of the station. It will be fun, interactive and entertaining. We will play more music than our (mostly talk) competitors."

As the show went through the normal "growing pains" any new show has, questions arose and conflicts emerged. Their interpretation of what was consistent with the demographic goals of the station didn't match mine. The relationship became strained and they felt I had lost confidence in their abilities. In reality, I had lost confidence in their execution of *my* concept of the show, which evolved into an unfortunate separation.

In retrospect, the talent reacted exactly the way they should be expected to react. I had not established the foundation on which to build the show, and they became frustrated because the only concrete, systematic standard of measure was Arbitron, the ultimate measure of performance. However, it's absolutely the *wrong* thing to judge a show or station's progress.

By taking the time to communicate better up front, and construct a useful, meaningful, and specific mission statement, this revolutionary new show could have shaken up the market and been on top today!

CHAPTER 4

11 HABITS OF HIGHLY EFFECTIVE SHOWS

One of the world's foremost consultants, Alan Burns, conducted an extensive study that compared the most prominent morning shows in America. The project found 11 traits that most of the shows shared.

t's impossible to concoct a formula that ensures morning show success, but through careful examination of the most successful shows in America, there are some common traits that most shows share.

This study includes an investigation into the success of a wide variety of morning shows in many formats, including Jeff & Jer (Star 100.7/San Diego), Rick Dees (KIIS/Los Angeles), Howard Stern (you know him), Dick Purtan (Station 3/Detroit), Paulson & Krenn (WDVE/Pittsburgh), Kidd Kraddick (KHKS/Dallas), Scott Shannon (WPLJ/New York), Mancow, and dozens more.

The startling discovery is that, regardless of format or target, most shows combined *most* of these 11 behaviors.

1. Leadership

Morning shows are leaders who direct and maximize their cast. The practice of directing starts with having a plan, an idea, a concept. The host keeps everyone in character and focused on the show. Rick Dees, Dick Purtan, Scott Shannon, and Howard Stern are perfect examples. You can hear it on these shows. They are always in command.

They also "maximize" their tools and resources by bringing out the best in their own talent and in his or her cast.

2. Clear Roles With Contrasting Viewpoints

Listen carefully to Howard Stern and Robin Quivers. Their contrasting personality gives dimension to the show and brings out the best in each other. Their characters and personalities are highlighted and strengthened because they are different. Jeff & Jer may sound similar to many, but they are vastly different personalities.

3. Not Just Topical, But Doing *Interesting* Things With Topics

This is the art of brainstorming and localizing to make an impact (see the chapter on Preparation).

Remember several years ago, when Bette Midler went off on Geraldo Rivera for claiming in his book that he slept with her? The morning after Bette Midler unloaded on a Barbra Walters special, the three major New York City morning shows all talked about the story. Z100's morning show mentioned the story, talked about it, and took some phone calls about it. Scott Shannon and Todd Pettengill on WPLJ went one step further. They had already produced a parody song, which got some reaction. But Howard Stern had Geraldo on the air in the studio that morning! Guess who won? Three different levels of involvement, three levels of doing something with the topic. Not coincidentally, the ratings shook out exactly the same way at that time: Stern beat Scott and Todd who were beating Z100's Zoo. To be fair, this was during the era that Z100 was without its big guns…after Shannon and Lander.

4. Making People Talk About You

There are many ways to create a "buzz" or word of mouth, and most are centered on appealing to an emotion. From outrageous opinions (Howard Stern) to humor (Rick Dees) to "I Can't Believe They Did That" (WNCI Morning Zoo, 99X/Atlanta) to stunts (Jeff & Jer, Mancow), talk-generating activity is GOOD.

5. One Large Benchmark

Find something you do very well, do it frequently, and make people remember you for it. Kidd Kraddick's philosophy is that morning shows are a series of "ones." If a show becomes known for one thing, it can be successful. For Larry Lujack, it was "Animal

Stories." Scott Shannon is known for his phone scams. John Lanigan does "Knuckleheads in the News."

6. Radio Theater

Throughout its history, our medium's traditional strengths have been immediacy, the ability to evoke emotion, and the ability to stimulate imagination. Remember *War of the Worlds*? How about the adventures of *Chickenman*? *Hiney Wine*? The material may be dated and the bits wouldn't "work" today, but the principles are timeless.

TV has co-opted the immediacy with satellites and mini-cams, but nobody can match radio's imagination and emotion. But, like a piano is just an instrument until a master pianist sits down, we often fail to play the right "keys."

Fewer and fewer people understand, believe in, or perhaps are simply willing to put in the effort to create fiction and theater in their morning shows. Though they probably don't realize it, too many morning shows seem to be practicing journalism (life as it really is) as opposed to entertainment (life as it could be). To reach out and touch the audience, we need to appeal to their sense of fantasy. Imagine an actor getting a call to join the cast of ER, but saying to the producer, "But, I'm not a doctor!"

7. Reflecting The Listener's World

Instead of dwelling solely in their own insular, self-absorbed world, great morning shows deal with the listener's world in entertaining ways. It's hard to go anywhere in Pittsburgh without having to drive through a tunnel, and tunnels always back up in morning and afternoon rush hour. While raving about WDVE's Paulsen and Krenn in a focus group, one of their fans said,

"They always talk about what I'm thinking about. For example, I was late to work this morning and I was getting frustrated in the back up at the Squirrel Hill Tunnel. As soon as I came out the other side of the tunnel and the radio came back on, there were Paulsen and Krenn, making fun of people who slow down at the tunnels."

8. Never "Above The Audience"

This is very closely related to the previous element.

Do you remember who the morning show was on KLOS before Mark & Brian? Probably not. Without naming names, the show's act basically consisted of being a star…or at least acting like a star. It was arrogant, intrusive, and self-absorbed. The show was a failure and no one remembers them. The audience rarely "listens up" to someone who thinks they're "all that."

9. Displays Of Emotion And Empathy

Again, one of radio's historic strengths as a medium is creating real, human emotion. Scott Shannon is one of the best at this. In fact, he's so good, he does it almost as a matter of routine. Becoming a personality that appeals on an emotional level is a skill that can be acquired through repetition. Keep working on it and it'll become much easier.

A few years ago, Kidd Kraddick had a phone call from a girl who grew up in Dallas, moved to Hollywood to try to become a star, and found herself working a succession of worse and worse jobs until she finally became a prostitute. One day she woke up, realized what she'd done with her life, packed her car, and started driving back to Dallas. En route, she called Kraddick in Dallas to tell him her story and how happy she was to be home. Kidd let her continue her story, she broke down and started crying during the call. The emotion may have been out of character for the basic sound of Kidd's show, but it was a tremendously powerful spike that made it a great story.

10. Playful, Affectionate Kidding

The audience doesn't just listen to the radio…they FEEL it. They pick up subtle clues in banter that sends a message of how the show feels about each other.

11. Longevity With Continued Commitment

One of Jeff & Jer's secrets to success is their advice to "find a market and marry it." It's hard to compete with market equity, provided the cast keeps working hard on the show. It's the longevity with continued commitment that makes the difference!

The highway is littered with shows that once were great, but declined when they stopped working hard. In this business, you can't mail it in. Greg Maddux is baseball's best pitcher, but if he decides he can win 20 games without committing to a work ethic, his success will be short-lived.

On the other hand, people like Shannon, Stern, Purtan, and Kraddick keep challenging themselves to reach greater heights. It's no coincidence that their success continues.

CHAPTER

5

UNDERSTANDING
THE
SHOW

I f a personality is expected to have a significant impact on the listening habits of the desired audience, it stands to reason that some energy be spent understanding the basis of what the show, audience, and station are all about. Looking at the radio through the eyes and ears of a listener reveals drastic differences about what we *thought* we *knew*.

Friends and family of anyone in the business are not normal listeners. The moment they know someone in radio, they listen differently. Closer, more critically. They remember more.

Talent Tip:
Talent should learn to disregard comments (positive and negative) made by those closer to the radio industry. That includes close friends, co-workers, and advertisers. They do not listen like real listeners!

The same goes for sales personnel and their clients. They're not normal listeners. Talent and PDs will field complaints from them constantly. Smart clients try to negotiate rates by complaining about the programming and talent. Complaints mean they are listening, and responding. The sales person should thank them for it, but usually they go to the PD and demand changes.

Any PD who uses acquaintances and friends as the source for programming will lose the respect of the staff, and rightfully so. The staff won't know who to please — the PD or his friends. The only important person to please is the listener. Smart programmers help the talent sift through all the clutter that constantly bombards them in the form of criticism and feedback.

Talent needs to be fearless in the studio, and know that the only goal is to make the station a winner. Talent is like an ace tennis player, and the PD is their personal coach. Each distraction is a mosquito on the court. Annoyed salespeople? Mosquito. Complaining GM? Mosquito. Listeners complaining? More mosquitoes. Not enough show prep or tools (in their opinion)? Mosquito. The PD's job is to keep the mosquitoes away. If the PD doesn't shield the talent, they will dwell on these small distractions and the show will drift off track. The talent doesn't even need to know about the conflicts. PDs should just take it, absorb it, and keep the talent confident and fearless on the air.

WHAT IS THE AUDIENCE ALL ABOUT?

Your market and your target audience have unique qualities that cannot be generalized. Your own market research will help identify these characteristics. Programmers should involve talent in some of the research process. Knowledge is power.

However, there are some "universals" about radio listeners, and it's helpful to understand what they are all about.

Let's start with radio in general. Contrary to what we'd like to believe, it just isn't important to real people. Mostly, they aren't paying attention to what station is on, not to mention WHO is on that station. Listeners tune in if it's convenient, if it fits their lifestyle. They won't go out of their way to participate. To be successful, you have to be user-friendly. Adapt to their lifestyle.

Since they're usually not attached to any station in particular, listeners are quick to punch out what they perceive as negative. They make quick decisions about what they like and don't like. Bad song? Punch out. Annoying commercial? They're gone. DJ that talks too much? See ya. Since they make such quick judgements, you have to get it right the first time. A new personality that is identified as a negative has a hard time making up lost ground.

> **Talent Tip:**
> Listeners will not change their lifestyle to listen to the radio, so your focus should be to fit your station into their lifestyle.

Listeners also are habitual. They listen in patterns. Their routine is nearly identical every day, often down to the MINUTE. You can become part of that routine with entertaining benchmarks that fit into their lifestyle daily, predictably. They won't change their lives to listen to you, so you have to make it easy for them to participate with you.

That's one reason why it's much better to image your station with something that has already happened than it is to pre-promote something coming up tomorrow. "If you missed today's show" promos are much more effective than, "Hey, guess what's coming up tomorrow." Listeners won't change their ritual to accommodate you. It's very difficult persuade them that

> **Talent Tip:**
> **Establish benchmarks in your show so you can become part of the listener's daily routine. Some of the most legendary morning shows became that way with years of consistency, to the point that listeners said "I know that when (talent) does the cash call at 7:20, I need to be on the freeway."**

what you have planned tomorrow is worth changing their routine. There's more information on that in the section about promoting the show.

Similarly, it's much better to tell listeners *exactly when* you want them to listen and what to do, than just to say, "Keep listening for your chance to win." Instead, say "Listen today at 1:45." Then tell them exactly what to do at that time! That works! It's much easier for a listener to participate if you give them a specific time to listen instead of "sometime between 10 and 5."

They listen for short periods of time, usually 20-30 minutes maximum, especially in the morning. Pre-selling something that won't pay off for more than half an hour doesn't make sense, does it? Tease your upcoming elements, pay them off quickly and move on.

Morning Show Research

"Market research has established beyond the shadow of a doubt that the egg is a sad, sorry product and it obviously will never sell. After all, eggs won't stand up by themselves, they roll too easily, are too easily broken, require special packaging, look alike, are difficult to open, and won't stack on the shelf."

-Robert Pliskin, VP, Benton & Bowles

So why do research? Well, as in sailing, it's much easier to adjust the sails than redirect the wind. The more you know about the audience, the more equipped you are to attract them to your show. While the above statement typifies what most talent feels about market research (and there is an important lesson to learn in that tongue-in-cheek comment), market research can be invaluable in helping to understand the audience.

A fortune has been spent researching radio listeners to try and find what they WANT in an entertaining air personality in general and in the morning show in particular. First, understand where your station fits in the list of priorities. Here are the Top 10 answers to the question, "What do you habitually do every morning?"

10.	Feed the pet	13%
9.	Iron Clothes	17%
8.	Read the Paper	27%
7.	Watch TV	42%
6.	Kiss their spouse	46%
5.	Make Breakfast	52%
4.	Exercise	53%
3.	Drink Coffee	56%
2.	Make the Bed	58%
1.	Listen to Radio	60%!!!!!!

That makes the radio in general, and your show in particular, pretty important, right? Not so fast! Read on!

THE IMPORTANCE OF RADIO

Take a look at the research table on the preceding page. Notice how listeners spend their time in the morning. The #1 activity is *listening to the radio*!

So, you're important right? Wrong. Try again. It's about as important as the toaster. You are a convenience, something they take for granted. They depend on you, for sure. But the radio is little more than a convenience that makes the chore of waking up and getting their day started a bit more bearable. Cutting through the clutter and becoming important enough to be remembered…to get their attention and their VOTE….is entirely different.

An interesting exercise is to ask a group of people a series of questions about brand names, things they purchase every day, such as laundry detergent, toothpaste, and deodorant. Most can name only 3-4 items in any product category. Then, ask them to name their favorite…they'll have one!

Now, ask them how many other brands are in that product category. They'll be amazed to know that there are 15-20 (or more) in each category. When you list them, they will recall using that product, and some will even admit it's the one they use *most*! Yet they didn't even mention it when asked initially.

It's the same with radio. Most listeners can name 8-10 radio stations, but listen to only 3-4 stations regularly. And, more importantly, the one they listen to *most* may be forgotten and not even register in their "top of mind" awareness.

Now, consider this: most products — even laundry detergent — have more importance in the life of listeners than radio stations. After all, they make a conscious decision to purchase and use these products. They have equity, a personal investment, in these consumer products. Radio is FREE, something that has no intrinsic value to them.

Finally, since ratings success is based only on top-of-mind recall, it is imperative to be *known*. If you don't get your station — or your morning show — to the upper part of your audience's consciousness, you haven't made the "sale." If a consumer buys Advil but doesn't remember, the makers of Advil still generate revenue and gain market share. But if they listen to your station but don't remember listening to it, you get nothing.

It's not enough to get them to listen…they have to KNOW they listened, and know WHO they heard! In other words, to be successful, personalities have to punch through the perceptual clutter and make an impact!

So the deck is stacked against your success before you begin. The only way to win is make the station and the show inseparable, important...and memorable! You have to become a part of their routine and adapt to fit their lifestyle.

More Morning Research

Further research shows how listeners rank various elements on morning shows. The question is,

"Which of the following elements are important to you in a morning radio show?"

1. A lot of music 39%
2. Entertaining DJs 35%
3. Weather Reports 29%
4. Traffic Reports 20%
5. News 19%
6. Information about local events 17%
7. Frequent news updates 16%
8. Crazy outrageous DJs 16%
9. Contests/Prizes 12%
10. Information about health 7%
11. Information about trends/fads 4%

Isn't it interesting that the information listeners can use right NOW, and that affects them PERSONALLY (weather and traffic) score so well? Both are ahead of NEWS. Keep that in mind as you organize and construct your show. You really can't deliver these substantial service elements too often. There's more detail on how to present news and traffic information in Chapter 15.

The respondents were also asked their preference for various morning show types. In all cases, we find that *personality* is what makes the difference in morning shows, but music plays a vital role. It's the "meal" that provides the substance. The

> **Talent Tip:**
> **Make useful information elements (weather, traffic, etc.) easily accessible and readily available to listeners.**

personality is dessert. A dining experience at a five-star restaurant wouldn't be satisfying without the main course (music), but you will most likely tell your friends about the dessert (personalities).

Personality makes the morning show happen, but in most situations you can't survive without some music presence.

WHAT PEOPLE SAY THEY WANT

Before you can appeal to a listener's orientation, you have to understand what is on their mind. Many shows entertain themselves instead of focusing on what's important to the listener. You've all heard these shows that are talking to hear themselves talk, and sound stuck on themselves.

We know what people SAY they want in a morning show, but what they REALLY want is quite different in many ways. Here's what they TELL us:

1. **No Talk.** This is a built-in bias against what most shows try to accomplish. It's strike one before you start. The audience has been conditioned to believe that all talk is bad…at least on a music station. Stations have dug this hole for themselves with years of "less talk, more music" advertising. Because of this, shows start from a perceptual "hole." What listeners really mean is they hate inane, meaningless, pointless talk that doesn't entertain them. So, make it pay off!

> **Talent Tip:**
> **Rule of thumb that settles a lot of debate on how much talk is too much: If what you're saying is more entertaining than the song you could be playing, it's not too long. If it's not, you have talked too much.**

2. A Mood. Radio listeners tune in to specific stations for specific reasons, mostly to get into a mood. They don't choose stations by the music they play, but by the mood the station creates. Of course, music is a large part of what creates the mood. Match their mood, win their loyalty. Most listeners have a station that they can relax to, that gets them going, etc. This emphasizes the importance of consistency and predictability. All of your material should go through a "filter" that supports the mood of the show, and the station.

3. Music. In general, they desire uptempo, familiar music. In most cases, music is STILL the #1 thing that listeners SAY they want in the morning. That doesn't mean talent is unimportant, and some shows can get away with less music than others. But it does point out the importance of maintaining a music presence in the morning show, especially in a station's growth phase. As a station's music image emerges, morning shows can mature as well, but must always remain conscious of the music demand of the listener.

4. Weather & Traffic. The service elements. Things I need to know NOW to plan for my day. News is NOT as important. Listeners want information they can use, that they can't get easily from other sources. The newspaper won't tell a listener how long it'll take to get to work today, but radio does. Even if there's nothing abnormal happening, it's the security blanket they need to plan their day, and it's your duty to give it to them regularly, consistently, and in an easy to digest manner. Give them the info, then get back to putting them in that mood again. By the way, traffic is more psychological reassurance that prepares listeners for what to expect, than actual information. That's why it's at least as important to tell them that "all's clear on your commute today" as it is to dispense information when there's a problem. Some stations go so far as to make weather and traffic a benchmark. Traffic is a great position to own if you can do it, and if it fits the overall station goals.

5. **News.** For most music stations, it's just the headlines, but it must be credible, relevant, and reliable news. Your key air personalities should NEVER deliver news. Be sure your audience knows what is going on in the world so they feel like they are in touch. Let them know what relevant things happened last night, and are likely to happen today. Be sure they don't feel out of touch with what their friends are talking about.

6. **Personality and Entertainment.** In most cases, it's the icing on the cake, not the main ingredients. Give them something to make them smile, make them laugh. Be a part of their life. Listeners tend to HATE trivial information and self-centered talk. The younger the audience, the less they say they want personality. Now, while listeners list the personalities LAST in importance, remember it's only what they SAY they want, not what they actually respond to. It's just another bias you have to overcome in making your show truly important.

QUALITATIVE RESEARCH

Quantitative research is effective for measuring awareness, recall, and some morning show images. However, focus groups are better suited for digging in and getting at the attitudes behind those responses. That's where you can really find out what people think about various shows. If your station conducts focus groups, each personality should be invited to watch, either live or on videotape. The experience will change the way they look at their role.

From years and years of focus groups covering hundreds of morning shows, here are a few basic conclusions that apply to most shows:

1. **Keep it simple.** Don't overdo it. One or two memorable things per hour are plenty, rather than a lot of smaller attempts. Spend a lot of time developing depth and more angles on one topic instead of constantly shifting gears and coming up with more material.

2. **People remember shows by ONE reference.** Remember Steve Dahl's disco demolition in Chicago in the 70s? Jeff & Jer's American Flag in the early 90s? Mancow stopping traffic on the bridge for a haircut? If you can find *one thing* that is tremendously memorable, you're on your way. Be KNOWN for something. Stay alert to the ONE thing you can do to get on the map. Think in "ones"...ONE truly GOOD bit per hour, one GREAT bit per show, one HUGE bit per market. Do that, and you'll be NUMBER ONE.

3. **Keep doing it.** There's a tendency to give up too soon. It takes time for listeners to catch on, longer to like it, and even longer to internalize it. So keep at it long after it no longer holds your fascination. When you've started thinking you've overdone it, they're just figuring it out! It's just like music. When the DJs can't stand hearing that song one more time, you know the audience is just starting to learn the words.

4. **Keep doing it the same way!** Don't change successful bits for the sake of variety. Letterman keeps doing his Top 10 in the same, successful way. It's better to ⊢ predictably entertaining than unpredictable, inconsistent, and "who knows if this will work."

Dropping a long-standing element simply because it's "old" reduces your memorability and disrupts habitual listening you've worked so hard to develop.

5. **Self-contained bits generally work better than long running bits that drag on over several breaks.** Remember how listeners use the radio. They listen in short bursts. Don't predicate your elements on the listeners having heard the last time you dealt with the bit. Set it up, pay it off. If you repeat it or continue it later, you have to reset the stage again.

6. **"Nice" shows usually finish last.** Controversy works better than relentless pleasantness. It's better to push the limit of the market, then not cross that line, than it is to chitchat. The best structure is multi-dimensional that has a personality that adds an edge, and other elements that have a heart.

7. **Content makes you successful, not style.** Howard Stern has a bad-boy attitude and style, but it's his content and talent, not his style, that make his show work

8. **Emotion is the key.** Joy, sympathy, empathy, anger, tragedy, tenderness, humor, rage, and patriotism all work! Your goal is to generate powerful responses and emotions from your listeners. Learn to appeal on an emotional level. See "Make Them Laugh, Make Them Cry" in Chapter 7.

Be Memorable

Ensure regularity. Use the same elements and features at the same time each day. Over time, listeners will be able to know what time it is by what is on the radio. Become a part of their lifestyle through consistency and training.

Daily Themes will help establish regularity and benchmarks. For example:

Manic Monday/Miserable Monday/Movie Monday
Trivia Tuesday/Name that Tunesday/No Pants Tuesday
Worst Joke Wednesday/Men Are Scum Wednesday
Threefer Thursday/Trash Thursday
Finally Friday/Free for All Friday

IDENTIFYING LISTENER TURNOFFS

Just as it's important to know what listeners desire in their morning radio listening, it's also essential to know what generally does NOT work. A great deal of your list for listener turnoffs will be common sense, and will be apparent when establishing your target audience profile and mission statement.

> *Talent Tip:*
> *Most morning shows work too hard on the air and should spend more time in developing fewer bits that have more impact.*

Still, there are several things to avoid, especially in a new show. These things may not make people dislike your show, but could prevent you from establishing your show quickly.

1. **Long Introductions.** Get right to the point. Set it up quickly and get right to the payoff with no detours. That's why you hear talk shows saying, "Carol in Pleasantville is next…what's on your mind, Carol?" instead of going through the introduction. Cut to the chase. A common technique is to start at the END of the bit, the punchline, then back up as far as you need to in order to paint the picture, or tell the story. Comedy writers have used this technique for stand-up monologues for years. Remember, listeners have a short attention span. You have to capture them quickly!

2. **Controversy.** Your show can be controversial, but should usually avoid BEING the controversy. Listeners don't react well to being psychologically tested. When listeners are made to feel uncomfortable, they punch out. Don't get in too deep with them. It's great to poke fun at controversial things and take opinions, but you should always do so in a way that is consistent with your personality and character development on the show. However, you should have a point of view. After all, if you stay in the middle of the road, the chances of being run over are doubled.

3. **Crude Talk.** Listeners respond to light, blue humor IF it fits the profile of the station. But, never cross the line of good taste as identified in your mission statement. Be cute, not crude. Fun and

playful, not vulgar and disgusting. Also, understand that listeners can get away with more than the personalities can. Let THEM say things that push the envelope....with your personalities' appropriate reaction, of course. Rick Dees is a master at taking a caller to the "scene of the crime, putting a club in their hand and letting them deliver the fatal blow."

4. **Too Much Production.** Too many elements become noisy and cause the message to be lost. The listener is over-stimulated and can't take any more. Fatigue sets in, and they tuneout. Production elements should accent your content, and make them stand out, not become the focus of the "bit." Too much production causes the listener to have difficulty distinguishing what they are supposed to be listening to. The morning zoos with wacky sound effects used to be huge, but don't work anymore.

5. **Too many characters.** Again, the important information gets lost. Listeners, who are only paying partial attention anyway, can't keep track of who's who on the show. Character development is impeded and character roles don't develop. If you have more than 2 or 3 regular personalities on the show, be careful. The personalities and roles must be distinct, unique, and offer diverse contributions. New characters should be introduced slowly, constantly reinforcing who they are and what role they play.

6. **Too many ideas.** Listeners just can't keep up with you if you throw out too many topics, bits, games, contests, and ideas in a short period of time. The show moves too fast, and gets uncomfortable. Most new shows tend to spend too much time preparing QUANTITY and not enough developing the QUALITY. Take a couple of great ideas and work them from every angle.

> **Talent Tip:**
> **Be careful not to add too many new elements or new voices to a show. Each character on the air must be well defined and add a new dimension to the whole.**

WHAT DO THEY REACT TO?

The building blocks of the show are the benchmarks that give you a foundation. Focus each element through your personality filter and mission statement. And do it consistently. Like Letterman's Top 10 list. Your show needs a centerpiece.

Remember, listeners find comfort in familiarity...familiar songs, and familiar personalities. The classic comedy shows of the past had a predictable punchline — Archie Bunker calling Michael "Meathead" or the gang in Cheers calling out "Norm" when George Wendt's character entered the bar. These simple hooks may appear insignificant. After all, they were never the topic of a script, but their presence gave their shows a framework and foundation while also developing personality traits for the characters.

Since listeners retain 2-4 unique things about your show, you only have to find a few things you do very well to get on the map. But you have to do those things well, and be creative in presenting them daily. Keep it simple. Make it easy to remember. You're in the top of mind game! It's better to hit one "home run" than five singles! The key is to become known for something that gets you shelf space in the mind of your listener. It's like the toothpaste that strives to be known for "whiter teeth."

> **Talent Tip:**
> Developing relevant "top of mind" awareness starts with focusing the show on making a significant point with one or two messages delivered in a wide variety of ways.

This leads to a very structured show, especially in the formative stages of your show. The key is to keep it sounding spontaneous and fun. Achieve "planned" spontaneity. Be predictably unpredictable within a comfortable and expected format.

When you find the unique elements that make you interesting, define them clearly and promote them well. Put everything you have into it! As long as they are interested in your topic, you can sell it to your audience and make it important to them. Remember, your listeners have short attention spans. There is room for repetition. Make it entertaining. Understand that, and use it to your advantage!

Repetition WORKS

To demonstrate the value of consistency and creative repetition in your show, it's important to understand the marketing principle of "Concentration of Force."

Successful marketers have proven that focusing all resources over a very short period of time with heavy concentration is much more effective in penetrating the awareness level of the target audience.

Here's a great illustration. Take an ordinary sheet of 8x10 paper, stretch it out between your hands and hold both ends tightly. Now, ask someone to place the palm of their hand in the center and push through the paper. If they can do it at all, it will be exceptionally difficult.

Now, ask them to take their index finger and poke the middle of the paper. It will penetrate the paper quickly and easily.

The lesson: Put all your effort into a narrow focus and concentrate on making an impact with your target. Spreading your resources over a broad range of efforts will fail to make an impression.

CHAPTER 6

YOUR
ON-AIR
CHARACTER

Once the PD and talent are on the same page philosophically, the battle is half over. Take the time to identify what the station and the show are all about. You also know what the AUDIENCE is thinking about. That's great. Knowledge is power. But, it's time to start making it happen on the air. Now the fun begins.

> **Talent Tip:**
> **Develop new shows slowly. It's easier to add more content later than it is to pull back.**

Whenever a new show is introduced, proceed with caution. Move slowly. It's easier to loosen control as time goes by than it is to impose new restraints after granting creative license. As you become more familiar and comfortable with the show and as the station grows, you can allow more responsibility. This also promotes the "trust" factor between you and the show.

Eventually, some programmers go so far as to allow the talent to essentially "program" their own show, in concert with overall station goals, of course. That's a privilege that must be earned! But then again, if the mission statement is properly constructed there's nothing to worry about. That's how stations go from "good" to "great." Everyone participates in the

> **Talent Tip:**
> **A station built on air talent that are merely "DJs" is like a basketball team built solely on great ball handlers. It's an important skill, but you need someone to put the ball in the basket!**

success and contributes to the building of your station. You get to be the conductor of this great orchestra! Give your talent equity in the station, a personal and professional stake in your success, and they will take care of the product for you!

In most cases, the morning show is mostly responsible for projecting the image your station has with the public. Don't let the morning show become an island, or separate entity unto itself. This takes a lot of hard work and dedication on your part, but it's essential in the long-term effectiveness of your station.

If you pay attention, and work on the relationship, you'll never wake up one morning and find that your company is considering a format change because the rest of the station can't keep up with prime dayparts.

DEVELOP CHARACTERS, NOT DJS

Who Are You? What Is Your Character?

There are as many personality types as there are successful personalities. Your shows will have their own unique attitude and personality as well.

Great air talent must know WHO they are, and have the confidence to deliver! From birth, you're developing a personality, a sense of being, a feeling about who (or what) you are. As you mature, your

> **Talent Tip:**
> *You can never compete with someone by becoming more like them.*

personality evolves. Your teenage years (and many young-adult years) are spent trying to "find" yourself.

The same is true in the life of an air talent. Assuming they are properly motivated and dedicated, the most important question they must answer is "Who ARE you?" What type of personality do you have? What is your point of view? How will you project that into successful air work? Air talent plays a "role" on the air, and it's important to know what that role represents.

In Chapter One, you learned that successful talent is not "fake." By that, we mean "not faking sincerity, interest in the audience or enjoyment of the show." Being "real" doesn't preclude *fiction* on the air. In fact, developing and refining your character almost certainly requires some degree of fiction. Remember, you wouldn't tell the producer of ER, "I'm not a doctor!'"

At Disneyland, there are no employment offices. They call it "casting." Everyone plays a role. They don't hire a janitor, they hire an actor playing the role of street sweeper. The radio application to this concept is simple. Everyone is an actor that plays a role in the station script. From the morning show to the person answering the phones to the van driver.

It's very important for the cast of the show to have clear characters that the audience can identify easily. The more differentiated the character roles are, the more creative tension is generated, and the more likely it will be that the listener will be able to personally identify with the show.

Think about any hit TV sitcom. It's easy to pinpoint the characters and their purpose easily. On *Seinfeld* there's a normal guy (Jerry) who usually succeeds, an attractive girl with all the problems of a single woman (Elaine), a madman who is always dreaming up bizarre ideas and situations (Kramer), and a pitiful loser (George). Would that show have worked if they all had the same character as Jerry?

Great talent must have a definite sense of what they are all about. Understand the ROLE and it will be much easier to perform and entertain. They sit down and describe exactly who they are and what they want to be. It's a natural extension of the show's mission statement, but becomes a more specific, descriptive characterization of the personalities. This will take some time. Here's an example:

Johnny Jock is both sophisticated and corny. He is slick at times, but often with a corny punchline. His delivery and approach reminds you of Letterman. Even when he's not putting you on, you still expect something to happen.

Johnny relies on listener input to keep the show going. Listeners feel they can contribute to the show anytime, anyplace. He is approachable, easy to talk to, and listeners feel he is their friend. Though the show often sounds spontaneous and unplanned, a great deal of preparation goes into each element.

Johnny never crosses the line of good taste himself, but will allow listeners and character voices to be off color. When they do, he reacts with surprise and disgust. Johnny knows that to be successful, he has to let others be the star sometimes.

Johnny is predictable, consistent and sincere. Listeners expect, and get, a good laugh. He never insults the listener or talks down to them.

What kind of personality will YOU be? A smart-ass, one liners type? Someone who hangs with the stars? Loose, controversial, opinionated, sarcastic, outrageous? Natural, real, familiar, comfortable? If you're nice, are you also goofy? Are you the guy everyone wants to hang out with? Has an opinion on everything? Cares about people? Does crazy stunts? To answer that question, you must KNOW who you are, and what your character represents. These must be similar, but not necessarily identical. Then, stay consistent and true to that persona.

Write down your personality and describe it in great detail. The worksheet on the next page will help you start. Then, memorize your character and *never* deviate. You must also know the character of every member of the show. Be sure each member is playing a role that is somewhat natural for them, and consistent with their real personality. Assign someone, usually the producer, the task of being the show's watchdog. Their job is to never let members of the show drift out of character. After all, no matter how well you can act, there must be some "realness" to your act.

IDENTIFYING PERSONALITY TRAITS

Here's a simple worksheet that will help start the process of developing a personality statement. This is a short list. There are hundreds of other possibilities.

Funny	**Outrageous**	**Corny**
Goofy	**Smart Ass**	**One-liners**
Off Color	**Dirty**	**Fun**
Sensitive	**Relatable**	**Real**
Sincere	**Caring**	**Friendly**
Outgoing	**On-the-Edge**	**Witty**
Concerned	**Dry**	**Droll**
Quick	**Clever**	**Quirky**
Off-the-Wall	**Spontaneous**	**Brash**
Chauvinistic	**Bold**	**Wimpy**
Opinionated	**In-touch**	**Reserved**
Confident	**Likes to Party**	**Daring**
Trustworthy	**Informed**	**Naive**
Crazy	**Zany**	**Dirty**
Out-Of-Control	**Off-color**	**Goofy**
Caring	**Comfortable**	**Cocky**
Sophisticated	**Predictable**	**Sarcastic**
Well-connected	**Hangs with Stars**	**Wild**
Controversial	**Approachable**	**Informed**
Enthusiastic	**Easy to talk to**	**Sensitive**
Does crazy stunts		

Defining Your Character

One way to help define characters on the show and help identify personality traits that can be exaggerated for maximum impact is also a lot of fun and will go a long way to helping the show bond.

Gather the talent, PD, producer, and anyone else who knows the talent well (including wives, close friends, etc.) in a room. Make a complete list of all the attributes of each person on the show, one person at a time. Write *everything* down. Is he/she: honest? A good cook? Afraid of spiders? Keep digging for more information.

When you've exhausted the list for each person, take a careful look at all of them. You'll find tons of opportunities to create character depth. For example, did one person grow up in a small town and another in a big city? Maybe you have your own "Green Acres."

Is one a hypochondriac, and the other the daughter of a doctor? (This actually occurred at a station.) That's another natural dynamic to accentuate. Keep looking for characteristics, attitudes, behaviors, history, and beliefs that can be fun if exaggerated and promoted, or played against the traits of others on the show.

ESTABLISHING YOUR CHARACTER

Now, how do you promote those traits on the air? More than ever, personalities are unique, different, and have less in common with other shows. Promoting your character on the air is much more subtle than promoting the show. The key is to find some little "hooks" to thread through the show that help listeners identify members of the cast.

However, there are some basics that are common, to give you a greater chance of making it in such a competitive world. Most great shows incorporate some degree of each of these. These should be considered your weapons of war in your show.

- **Listener Contact.** A feeling that this is a public forum. The show is designed from the outside in, instead of inside out. Listeners are the lifeblood of most shows. The way the talent reacts to and relates to the listeners will further establish characters.

- **Relatables. Local and emotional.** The advantage over syndicated shows is that you can tap into your community mood and reflect those attitudes, mindsets, and lifestyles in YOUR City. How you choose to react to local events will say much about who you are on the air.

- **Talk Stimulators.** Shows that win usually find a way to create "water cooler" talk. Get listeners to remember what you do and create reasons for them to talk about your station. And, more importantly, get them to talk about you in a way that promotes your desired image.

- **Characters.** Again, something relatable and memorable. The more unique and distinct, the better. Any drop-in characters on the show provide content, but also an opportunity to position a talent's characteristics by how they respond to the characters.

- **A Great Laugh.** A sincere laugh can make it sound fun. People like to be with people having a good time, and laughs become contagious. HOW you laugh and WHEN you laugh add to your character. Great laughs go a long way.

- **Anticipation.** Tease it. Use theater of the mind. Build up the drama. Casey Casem is a master at this.

- **Mental Interaction.** Involve and challenge your listeners. Engage them in your show.
- **Cinematic Production.** Stimulate the imagination. But don't let the production elements overtake the content. Make it dramatic to emphasize key moments.

Stay True To Your Character

Once you've established a firm expectation for your show, stick with it! Rick Dees is a "funny nice guy." That's what his listeners expect from him. When Howard Stern first came into Los Angeles, and generated all the press, Rick became jealous.

Soon, Dees was doing angry, controversial material in an attempt to win back the spotlight. It wasn't what his audience wanted or expected from him, and his ratings immediately plummeted. As soon as Rick got back on track again, the "funny nice guy" returned to his previous rank.

TOOLS TO DEVELOP CHARACTER

When developing those traits that set them apart, successful personalities use three essential tools:

Banter. There is a huge difference between banter and pointless talk, but also a fine line between the two. Banter has a purpose, a direction. It can be used to project a mental image of personalities into "characters." Well-defined "banter" makes you a meaningful personality by developing a bond with the listener. It gives them a chance to relate to a personality, or at least an aspect of the personality's character. The TV classic "Cheers" was written in brilliant banter. The characters all took on identifiable, relatable personalities because of the purposeful talk, well written scripts, and exceptional character development. Viewers got the feeling they knew everything about the characters' lives because of the exceptional banter.

WARNING: It is easy to cross that fine line and turn well-intentioned banter into a negative that leads listeners to feel "they didn't give me anything." Be careful not to drift into meaningless talk about yourself.

Surprise. Catch the audience off-guard occasionally with something unpredictable, off the wall, outrageous, or unexpected. BUT, it has to stay within your personality. Create the feeling of "I can't believe what they've done now...but it's just like them to do it."

> **Talent Tip:**
> There is a fine line between meaningless talk and constructive banter. Banter helps develop characters and define roles. But, even character building banter has to have a payoff to the listener.

Repetition. In order to teach someone a behavior, you must keep telling them what you want them to learn in many different ways. It's just like teaching your first-grader math facts. Repetition! Re-run great bits several times. Re-create great moments from your shows in promos. Keep developing the character and key points you want your audience to "learn."

Production. Produce "stagers" that make fun of, or exaggerate, various elements of the characters on the show. For example, "The XXXX morning show, starring _____, (city's) biggest hypochondriac, _____, the pyromaniac, and _____, the nympho...uh, never mind...Here they are."

Recurring Bits. Construct clever, interactive contests that the audience can participate in that help identify the show's characters. One is "Whose life is it?" Start with a clue about one of the cast member's lives (this cast member set fire to his father's Oldsmobile when he was five). The audience is invited to guess who it is.

SECTION 2

THREE STEPS
TO A
SUCCESSFUL SHOW

(Preparation — Concentration — Moderation)

By this time, you've determined what the show should sound like and are ready to put it on the air, right? Not so fast. Now that you're ready to go, how do you do it? How do you go from "drawing board" to "on the air"? Even the few morning shows that have thought their show and station through this far often fail to put the rest of the show together logically.

Great shows sound spontaneous, like you never know what they're going to do next. Like they don't know what they're going to do next.

But just like great actors and actresses seem to be so natural and real in the roles they portray, great air personalities are prepared, organized, and understand their purpose on the air. Without the proper structure, the best personalities in America don't have a chance to be successful.

One of the all-time great air talents AND outstanding programmer, Scott Shannon, teaches three steps to putting together a show: **Preparation, Concentration, and Moderation.**

The first phase, preparation, is the art of gathering information. Concentration is the process of focusing the material, the execution phase. Moderation is where you exercise discipline, restraint, and common sense. It's knowing when to say "when," and when to push further.

PREPARATION

"I can't say there isn't an ego boost or a higher sense of confidence in yourself when you have had as many lights shining on you as I have had. But I never believed all the press clippings and I never found comfort in the spotlight. I don't know how you can and not lose your work ethic."

— Michael Jordan, 1999

I CAN'T SAY THERE ISN'T AN EGO BOOST
OR A HIGHER SENSE OF CONFIDENCE IN
YOURSELF WHEN YOU HAVE HAD AS MANY
LIGHTS SHINING ON YOU AS I HAVE HAD.
BUT I NEVER BELIEVED ALL
THE PRESS CLIPPINGS AND
I NEVER FOUND COMFORT
IN THE SPOTLIGHT.
I DON'T KNOW HOW YOU CAN AND
NOT LOSE YOUR WORK ETHIC.

MY LIFE AS JOE BOB BRIGGS

The following excerpt is from the article "My Life As Joe Bob Briggs," found in the July, 1990 issue of Texas Monthly Magazine. The subject is comedy and the premise is that spontaneity sucks. The application to radio shows is to reinforce the need for careful planning and preparation.

After I was on The Tonight Show the first time, people would come up and say, "Wow! You and Jay Leno really hit it off! You had a great rhythm going on out there. Did you know what he was going to ask you?"

I'm tempted to say "Yeah, I was winging it that night. I was hot! Jay was hot. Everything was clicking for us. We could have gone on like that all night."

The truth is, and I feel shameful for doing this, like a magician telling how Houdini did his tricks, but the truth is that every guest on The Tonight Show goes through a phone interview with a producer, one of whom is named Jim McCawley. Jim's been doing this for thirteen years. And he says, "So, if Jay asked you this, what would you say?" And you say something incredibly witty and Jim goes, "Hmmm, okay, yes." And you hear him writing things down. Occasionally he'll say, "Nope. Can't do that. Not on the network." And so, unless you're Sam Kinnison and have a death wish, you don't do that joke on the show.

On the night of the show, actually the afternoon, since it's taped at 5:30, Jim gives both the host and the guest a sheet with questions and approximate answers. Every once in awhile you stray from the list, as I did the second time I was on the show, but only for brief periods. You always go back to the list, and you always say approximately what you said to Jim McCawley on the phone.

Of course, the greatest moments in television, like the greatest moments in life, are spontaneous, unforeseen, unprepared, unscripted. So why don't talk shows encourage those moments? Because, even for the great ones, it's impossible to do that every time out. A true ad-lib that is funnier than prepared material is like improvisation in music. Rarely is there a truly original jazz riff, for example. Once in awhile Dizzy Gillespie plays something that has never been heard in a long time, but most of the time he simply does a great job of playing the same song a little bit differently night after night.

PREPARATION. IT'S EVERYTHING.

Before you prepare your material, you must prepare yourself. Take the time to understand your audience and your station.

This starts with the process of analysis before making any key decision. On June 25, 1876, General George Custer received information that a significant number of Indians were gathering at Little Big Horn. Without analyzing the facts, he decided to ride out with 250 men to "surround" nearly 3,000 Indians. This was a serious mistake.

Stations and shows MUST prepare strategically before they prepare tactically.

A successful morning show must have a sense of organization, purpose, and direction!

Without a road map, the show is unlikely to reach a destination. At the core of morning show organization is the discipline to consistently review your goals and purpose. You should review the morning show objectives and organization at least once a month.

It all begins with your audience, and how your audience perceives you. Understanding your purpose and direction requires intimate knowledge of your target audience. Not just your demographic target, but your *psychographic* target. A good first step is to list the Top 10 topics for, and Top 10 activities of, your audience. What are their concerns? Worries? What makes them happy? How do they spend their time? Have every member of the show do their own, then compare notes. Come up with THE list. This gives you a great place to begin to organize elements that appeal to the target. Establishing that emotional bond with your listener starts with your organizational efforts.

Talent Tip:
Identifying your audience is like filling out a scouting report. You have to find out everything there is to know about them.

Be careful not to make subjective assumptions in this critical area. It's hard work to *find out* about your audience. One station in the dance format assumed everyone in the audience went to clubs continuously, but when they really dug into the qualitative data available on the station, they found that their highest indexing activity was shopping at Woolworth's!

Talent Tip:
You can't be fully prepared
unless you first know
who you are preparing for.

Consider how the show is to be positioned on the station, and in the market, relative to other morning shows. What is the attitude, mood, and point-of-view you plan to portray? How do you want the audience to perceive you? Position the show just as you would the station. It's a marketing project. Make a marketing plan, and stick to it.

Remember The Listener

All the mental preparation and homework in the world will help get the show off in the right direction with the right intention. But when it's early in the morning, and the rest of the station is dark and quiet and the phones aren't ringing, it gets lonely in the studio.

That's when it's so easy to lose focus on *who* the listener really is. Many stations have helped the talent focus by creating a composite of the quintessential target listener.

Start with a large silhouette of the listener…the bigger the better. Then, inside the silhouette, attach photos of target-demo examples in activities they commonly participate in. Make it a staff project and get everyone's input and participation. This not only helps get them involved in the programming, but increases the chances of the finished work actually being used.

Put the project in a "can't miss" spot in the studio, and work with everyone on the staff to understand all they can about everyone in the photos.

Then, when the studio is lonely, the talent can pick out one of the examples and focus on talking just to that one person. One to one. Individually. This takes some practice and discipline, but it works!

The next step is to determine the role of each member of the show. This needs to be defined clearly and in advance of the show's debut. Is each personality on the air unique, and do they provide something the audience will relate to? If not, why are they on at all? Too many shows consist of a collection of people who *like* each other, and *are like* each other. That may make good chemistry on the weekend, but not in the studio.

> **Talent Tip:**
> **Putting together talent for a show is more like "casting" a play. You have to ignore the personal information and focus on the roles being filled.**

Who is responsible for what on the air? Who takes care of off-air concerns? Many shows tend to let everything work itself out, which rarely happens with good results. That doesn't mean that roles and personalities won't evolve and develop in a different direction. Evolution is good…properly managed, it leads to growth. However, disorganized evolution is deadly.

Some of the questions that have to be answered about the show include:

- **Who calls the shots in the studio?**
- **Who starts most of the breaks, and acts as the "anchor"?**
- **Who answers the phone?**
- **Who runs the controls?**
- **What are the producer's main responsibilities?**
- **Who is responsible to deliver station formatics and promos?**
- **Who keeps the show moving forward and "on time"?**
- **What are the character traits and attributes of each person's role?**
- **How is that role unique and different from all the other characters?**
- **Who keeps track of the show to be sure all members are staying within their role?**

The show also needs to know exactly what to expect from each other, and from the station. Post a schedule. What time does each member arrive? What are their duties each day? Who does the show prep? When? How about promos and post-production? When are off-air morning show meetings? When is the review/critique session scheduled? What days do you meet with the PD? Brainstorming? Follow through? Who keeps track of the appearance and social schedules? Who is responsible for internal communication with other dayparts and departments, especially sales and promotions? Who records the TV shows and edits them for sound bites the next day?

There are dozens of questions to answer, and nothing should be left to sort itself out. Issues you leave to resolve themselves rarely do.

This is the work ethic that separates the good shows from the great ones. Tony Gwynn has won more batting championships than any other player, but the key to his success is the hours and hours he spends watching tape, studying pitchers, and fine-tuning his stroke. It's a daily routine that keeps him at the top of his game.

DARE TO BE DISCIPLINED

Like great athletes, great shows are disciplined. In Latin, the word "disciplined" means to teach, to guide and instill inner control. Being fundamentally disciplined is something most shows don't want to talk about. But discipline and fundamentals are vitally important to any show.

One of the disciplines is service information, such as time, weather, and traffic information. It's important that listeners know these things frequently. And it's not enough just to DO it. It has to be "heard" by the audience. Many times the talent just "throws away" the information with little emphasis or sense of importance.

It's also vital to constantly reintroduce themes, topics and bits. Remember, people are only partly paying attention. They're laying in bed, or they are in the bathroom, shaving, showering, fixing breakfast, getting kids ready for school, a thousand tasks every day. It's a constant series of tune-in and tune-out.

> **Talent Tip:**
> If the show doesn't sound spontaneous, you probably haven't prepared enough.

To cut through this "brain clutter," you must give purpose to your breaks, to make it easy for listeners to follow along. Features, interviews, games, contests, information elements, and station promos all compete for attention and become "lost" if you don't manage the clutter and help listeners sort it out. Constantly pre-sell and tease what you have coming up. Brand your elements with your station call letters and show name when possible. Make it memorable, and keep it simple.

The discipline of fundamentals is part of the whole of creativity and content, but they are at opposite poles. It's not fun to keep going over the basics, just like it's not fun for baseball players to constantly practice bunting. The greatest success comes from balance and achieving "planned" spontaneity along with consistency and dependability. Winning comes when you combine individual creative sparkle with consistent fundamentals.

THE DAILY ROAD MAP

In Dallas, morning legend Kidd Kraddick has a rule for his show. "No winging it." He insists on preparing two major bits per hour. They can be dropped if things are rolling, but they must be on the schedule with a well-conceived plan to launch each bit.

A daily "road map" will keep everyone on track. Everyone needs to know what to expect and have a sense of where the show is going. Once on the air, detours are allowed, as long as the departure is better than the original plan, and the entire cast is aware of the substitution in advance. That doesn't mean the show is a democracy, with equal votes. It just means everyone needs to know what's happening. You should also be alert to get back on the "main road" following the detour, and don't allow the show to spin out of control aimlessly.

In the early days of the show, the program director should meet with the show daily to review the show and have input into the road map. His or her role is to keep the show focused and fulfilling the objectives all have agreed on. In other

> **Talent Tip:**
> Whether in business, sports or on the air, it's the little things, performed consistently and with excellence that will win over time.*

words, fix it before it breaks. This technique can be tremendously successful in helping shows hit their stride quickly and stay on target for what is truly important (fulfilling the mission statement). It also gives the PD a chance to come up with ways to maximize elements and promote the show on other dayparts.

The daily road map must be specific. However, don't be a slave to the outline. You have to be flexible enough to change course when a bit isn't working, or keep going longer when it is.

Use a planner/organizer that breaks down each hour and each quarter hour, and each break. Keep a week's worth of schedules in front of you to be sure that you balance material each day and each hour. A well-done planner will show you if you have enough of every type of bit. You'll be able to quickly identify a need for more listener-oriented features, humor, etc.

The Daily Road Map is different from a format clock in that it contains your ideas and concepts, not the mechanics of execution. The format clock is much more specific. Examples of both are in this chapter.

Notice how the daily planner leaves a lot of room for notes and alterations. It's a great resource to begin planning *tomorrow's* show.

THE DAILY ROAD MAP

Day _____   Date _____

Earlier This Week
_____

Coming up Later This Week
_____

_____

Coming up Next Week
_____

_____

Today:

<u>6-7 am</u>:   Major Bit:

                  Minor Bit:

                  Filler 1:

                  Filler 2:

                  Phone Topic:

NOTES:

7-8 am: Major Bit:

                            Minor Bit:

                            Filler 1:

                            Filler 2:

                            Phone Topic

NOTES:

8-9 am: Major Bit:

                            Minor Bit:

                            Filler 1:

                            Filler 2:

                            Phone Topic

NOTES:

9-10 am: Major Bit:

                            Minor Bit:

                            Filler 1:

                            Filler 2:

                            Phone Topic

NOTES:

What did we miss today that can be used tomorrow?

GETTING READY: GATHERING INFORMATION

Now that you have a structure, you have to have great material to fill those breaks. This is much more than just being aware of what's going on in the world around you. It's having a keen sense of how these events affect your target demographic. Then, finding a way to relate to those emotions will unlock what connects you with the audience.

The process of preparing the show each day starts with gathering information. There are a lot of ways to do it. Scott Shannon carries a recorder everywhere he goes. He reads everything, watches everything. He observes constantly.

Ross Britain over-prepares the day before, and is the best at preparing written material. He carefully collects data and structures each break for every show.

Jeff & Jer don't spend much time at the station, but tap into the lifestyle of the audience by living that lifestyle. They do the things listeners do and bring it to the air. They understand that to be effective on the air, you must have a wide enough sphere of interests to not always be "talking shop." They're a perfect example of a show living in the listeners' world.

Bob Rivers puts together a list of hot topics each day.

But show prep is a lot more than getting the information, or reading and reciting USA Today. If all you do is read out of the paper, you not only fail to entertain, but your audience will quickly realize that you're unoriginal, boring and not giving them anything they don't already know. That's LAZY, and it's a way to make yourself obsolete.

A major part of preparation is communication. Talk to each other about topics and material for the next day. Most great shows talk several times a day after they leave the station.

LOCALIZE

Show prep is a LIVING. It's spending your entire life paying attention. Everyone has access to the information. The difference between good shows and great shows is what you do with the information.

Preparing your show means localizing. That doesn't mean it has to happen in your local area. It means it has to be interesting to your market. When you hear a national or regional story of interest, don't just talk about it…relate it to your HOME. You read the story about the woman thrown out of her church for singing badly? Call and have her give you a sample, then ask your listeners to call and rat out people in their church who sing badly.

The process of show prep means going the extra mile and finding the angle that makes it more than just a "story." It means *telling* a story. Be a descriptive storyteller. Embellish your material with local references. Indulge your audience by talking about them, and where they live.

For example, instead of saying "I was driving down the road…" add descriptive detail that references local landmarks. Something like "While driving down Main street…and passing the clocktower…" Where you were driving may carry no significance to the bit you are developing, but it does two important things: It makes you local, giving you a point of reference for your audience, and it helps you paint a picture in their minds. They can identify and relate to the story with detail.

The art of being a great air talent is developing your story telling skills. Practice with children. Notice how much more interest is generated when you dress up stories, add sound effects, change vocal pitch, etc. When you relate to a child on their level, instead of telling them a "once upon a time," you capture their imagination. It's the same with your listeners.

Localizing Is A Commitment

What does it take to prepare to go on the air at a new station or new market for the first time? It takes commitment.

Before Jeff & Jer began their ratings dominance of San Diego in the late 80s, they spent several weeks getting to know the market. They explored the neighborhoods, visited the major malls, and drove the freeways, learned to pronounce the names of the streets and suburbs. In short, they did their homework so they wouldn't sound ignorant about the lifestyle of the audience they were trying so hard to seduce.

If you want listeners to consider you their "friend" they first have to consider you "one of them." That doesn't mean you should pretend you've lived in their market forever, but you have to communicate that you love their city and plan to make their market your home.

There is a certain charm about asking listeners for help in adjusting to their town as well. Many shows have created tremendous segments asking listeners to tip them off on where to go for a hamburger, the best place for happy hour, the best way to spend a weekend, etc. But that only works if you have already established that you are adopting their town as your own.

There are no shortcuts to living the lifestyle of your listener, especially in a new market. Spend time getting to know the people, their attitudes, tendencies. Find out what time they go to work, where the traffic gets bad (and when). Talk to clerks, waiters, hair stylists, and city workers. Find out what makes the city "tick."

Above all, never mispronounce a suburb, neighborhood, or street. There is no faster way to alienate an audience than to sound out of touch with their town!

PERSONALIZE

To communicate on an emotional, personal level with your target audience, you must know what's happening in their lives each day. You must know everything there is to know about your audience and what they are doing. Live in THEIR world. Incorporate the day-to-day aspects of the market and your audience into the show. How do you do it? Make it your passion to:

- **Observe.** Tune into what's going on around you. Carry a notebook and take notes on the little, mundane things that happen in your audience's lives. If your target is an audience that likely has school-aged children, know when school is out and relate to that. Notice little things in your area that affect your listeners.

- **Schmooze.** Get to know the movers and shakers in your community. Know the important personalities in your market.
- **Make lists, especially topic lists.** Pay attention to what is being addressed in TV shows. Know what happened in the most-watched TV shows.
- **Rent the new videos** that come out, and know what is being released.
- **See the hottest new movies** the week they come out, or at least know enough about them to ask intelligent questions of your listeners who have seen them.
- **Live the lifestyle of your audience.** If not actually, then mentally. Live life through their eyes and their experiences.
- **Know the streets** in the areas of town your audience is likely to reside. Nothing labels you an outsider faster than mispronouncing names of major streets, suburbs, or freeways.
- **Listen to listeners.** What do they say? What do they care about? What concerns them? Ask questions.

Post a checklist in your office to be sure that you are "in touch" with your community. Review it every single day so you never miss something. Update these questions daily:

1. What local events are coming soon, within the next two weeks?
2. What are most people in our target audience talking about today?
3. What is today's biggest news story?
4. What kind of day is it today? What is the mood, feel of the day?
5. What is my audience doing right now? Tonight?
6. What is the most talked-about new movie?
7. What TV show is hot right now…what's the best thing on TV tonight? Last night?
8. What have listeners said lately that we can use and reflect on the air?

If you can't answer these questions easily, without checking a reference, the show isn't prepared.

How Well Do You REALLY Know Your Audience?

Many entertainers *think* they know their audience, and assume they understand the demographic and psychographic well enough to effectively personalize their material. However, on further inspection, most fall short and are surprised when they get a dose of reality.

This article first appeared in a February, 1999 issue of Network 40 Magazine and was written by the magazine's editor and former CHR programmer, Gerry Cagle. It'll make you think again about how well you *really* know your audience.

Reality Check

by gerry cagle

We all pride ourselves by being on the cutting edge. No matter what is going on, we know everything about it. We can tell a hit from a stiff long before the record is set for release. You want to talk programming? I've got your programming right here!

This Editorial is about those of us who still believe we're on the cutting edge. We work harder, longer and smarter than the others. Remember when you first started? There was no job too small for you to do. You were the first in the parking lot and the last to leave. And on weekends, you were at station promotions or hanging at showcases just to soak up the atmosphere... learning along the way.

Then you got promoted. You may have gotten married and started a family. You took up hobbies like skiing, golf or tennis. And slowly, all the things you used to do that made you successful began to go by the wayside. It was difficult to find time in your now busy schedule for the little nuts and bolts that made you run smoother than the rest.

You began to slip.

Of course, I'm not talking about you. I'm talking about the other people. You're still on the cutting edge. Besides, it doesn't matter. You paid your dues. So what if you don't work quite as hard as you used to? You still are better than the rest. Suppose you are a little older. You still know exactly what your audience likes. You know the young consumer. You might be a little older, but you're hip. You're just like them.

Oh, yeah? Are you ready for a little reality check? Each year, the staff at Beloit College in Wisconsin puts together a list to try and give the faculty a sense of the mindset of that year's incoming freshmen. Here are a few gems from this year's list.

The people who are starting college this Fall across the nation were born in 1980.

They have no meaningful recollection of the Reagan Era and did not know he had ever been shot.

They were prepubescent when the Persian Gulf War was waged.

Black Monday 1987 is just as significant to them as the Great Depression.

There has been only one Pope in their lifetime. They can only remember one President.

They were 11 when the Soviet Union broke apart and do not remember the Cold War.

They have never feared a nuclear war. *The Day After* is a pill to them,

> "The people who started college this year were born in 1980."

not a movie.

They are too young to remember the space shuttle blowing up.

Tienamen Square means nothing to them.

Their lifetime has always included AIDS.

Bottle caps have always been screw off and plastic.

Atari pre-dates them, as do vinyl albums.

The expression, "you sound like a broken record," means nothing to them.

They have never owned a record player.

Most have never played Pac Man and have never heard of Pong.

Star Wars looks very fake to them and the special effects are pathetic.

There have always been red M&Ms and blue ones are not new.

They may have heard of an 8-track, but never actually seen or heard one.

The Compact Disc was introduced when they were one-year-old.

They have always had an answering machine and call waiting.

Most have never seen a TV set with only 13 channels, nor have they seen a black-and-white TV. They've always had cable.

There have always been VCRs, but they have no idea what BETA is.

They cannot fathom not having a remote control.

They were born the year that Walkmans were introduced by Sony.

The Tonight Show has always been hosted by Jay Leno.

They have no idea when or why Jordache jeans were cool.

They have never seen Larry Bird play and Kareem Abdul-Jabbar is a football player.

They never took a swim and thought about *Jaws*.

The Vietnam War is as ancient history to them as WWI or WWII.

They have no idea that Americans were ever held hostage in Iran.

They don't know who Mork was or where he was from.

They never heard: "I'd walk a mile for a Camel," "Ze plane...ze plane," or "Where's the beef?"

They do not care who shot J.R. and have no idea who J.R. is.

Michael Jackson has always been white. Kansas, Chicago, Boston and America are places, not groups.

There has always been MTV.

Does that "cutting edge" you're sitting on feel a little dull? □

e d i t o r i a l

The Magazine That Brought You Plays Per Week

NETWORK40

DAILY SHOW PREP

Preparing for each show takes a lot of time and effort. Some of the best air personalities spend two hours a day in preparation for each hour on the air. Many personalities are terrible at show prep. After all, it's a tedious, repetitive process and requires commitment every day to prepare properly. If that's the case, you have to find someone who can fill that role.

If you can master the process of preparation, through organizing your time and resources, you can greatly reduce the time it takes to put it together. It also helps to assign various prep sources to several members of the show.

COLLECTING DATA

With today's technology and ready access to information, it's easy to get the data. In addition to the obvious sources (newspapers, magazines, etc.), there are hundreds of sources that provide great ideas and thought-starters.

Don't get hung up on the pride of authorship. If someone else has done something that works, adapt it to your show. Borrow like a banshee. Be humble.

> **Talent Tip:**
> FORCE someone to surf key sites on the internet for material each day.

Use everything you get your hands on. Even joke books are great resources if you use them right. Bob & Tom have done this for years. They start with a joke and work it into something relevant in the lives of their listeners. The proper work ethic and relentless concentration on their show turn normal jokes into something personal and emotional.

Save everything. Phone calls, drops, ideas for bits. Everything is useful at some point. Use phone calls and listener drops out of context. Assign someone the task of maintaining a library of resources.

Here are just a few common resources to collect information and material for a show:

ONLINE SERVICES

Start with a good online service that other morning shows contribute to daily. They are inexpensive, and provide dozens of pages of material each day. Be sure to localize the ideas to your show.

If you don't have an internet account, get one. There are thousands of great websites that can be easily adapted for radio. Surf the net for humor. Be sure to bookmark the best sites and visit them as part of your daily routine. Usually you can "cut and paste" the best parts. The faster your connection, the better, and if you have access to cable modem technology, get it. It's terrific for downloading audio.

There's a list of great show prep sites to start with in the back of this book.

TELEVISION

Run a video tape daily on all the most popular shows, and of course any specials. This takes a lot of editing and time. But it pays off. It's the little things that make you better than your competition. They might be talking about last night's episode of the hottest new TV show, but YOU have the highlights! Big difference. This is part of the work ethic that separates you from competitors.

MOVIES

Rent movies and lift drops, but only the most familiar, hottest movies available. Stay away from random, unfamiliar drops that have no reference point. Play the hits! Establish relationships with movie companies to get on their mailing list for the promo trailers of their new movies. You can get great clips, ready for air. And don't forget to get on the web site of hot new movies. You can usually get audio clips of the most memorable/promotable parts of upcoming releases. Use these clips creatively to promote your show, your station, and your position. Or, use them to enhance information elements during your newscasts or entertainment reports. Tons of uses!

LOCAL TALENT

Visit the comedy clubs and karaoke bars, scouting for talent that can do song parodies, voices, or commentary for little or nothing. You'd be surprised what you can find, and they love the exposure you can give them.

MAGAZINES

Read the magazines your audience reads. Subscribe to them. Relate to them. Use the ideas on your show and make them your "own." You can take virtually any topic and brainstorm it into something new, fresh, and relatable for your audience.

UNUSUAL SOURCES

There are dozens of other sources you probably don't even know exist. Look for opportunities to collect publications for specific industries. Many will put you on their mailing list for free. Turn to the "letters to the edit or" pages and you'll find raging topics and controversial viewpoints on a wide variety of issues. When you find something new to you, list all possible ideas that come to mind. See the next section for examples.

There is no such thing as "luck" when it relates to success. Great ratings come from hard work, diligent work. It takes a relentless pursuit of excellence and an intelligent application of the information. Don't shortchange your listener. Be prepared and bring your best to the studio every morning!

To paraphrase Joe DiMaggio, "There may be someone listening that has never heard you before."

BRAINSTORMING IDEAS FROM UNLIKELY SOURCES

Brainstorming is an art. It's hard work, but it's also a lot of fun, and it can be very satisfying. Anyone can be creative if you put in the time. When brainstorming ideas, be sure to go one step further and add the local flavor.

Dan O'Day is a major proponent of creative brainstorming sessions, and offers an example of how to brainstorm a "bit" from a very unusual source, Frequent Flyer magazine. Note how you can take virtually any information and turn it into something useful on the air. In Phase I of brainstorming, start by compiling a list

> **Talent Tip:**
> **Practice brainstorming regularly until the thought process becomes second nature.**

of topics. Phase II is the local, personal, emotional angle you use to make the bit come alive.

In the "Letters to the Editor" section, a reader writes about the height, width, and legroom of seats on United planes. Here are topic possibilities that arise from this one letter:

- What was your worst plane ride ever?
- If I could design my own plane, what would it be like?
- Which airlines are the most comfortable? Best food?
- What's the dumbest thing I ever heard or saw on an airplane?
- What do you have to have to enjoy a great flight?
- What is the scariest moment you've had in a plane?
- What is the worst airport? Best airport?
- Stories about traveling with infants/pets/kids/senior citizens?
- What is the best strategy for keeping the seat next to you empty, for more legroom?

Another letter is from an airline employee who says that at the airport, the Gate Agent is GOD. She says her husband gets upgraded because of how he treats them.

- How can you get upgraded for free?
- Who is the most powerful person in your company?

• What are stories about nepotism in the workplace?

A third letter is a complaint about the quality of USAir's Priority Gold Plus membership for frequent fliers. Ideas:

• What's the best perk you've ever had in a job?

• What is the biggest misconception about your job?

• What services are getting worse? Banks, gas stations, etc?

• Have you ever gotten positive reactions from complaining about something?

The next letter is a from a reader outraged at paying $200 per night for a hotel room and still being charged for dialing 800 numbers from his room. Here are some thought-starters:

• Stories of people who have abused expense accounts?

• What's the worst rip-off in daily life?

• What dumb thing have you bought?

You get the idea. It doesn't take long to build up a bank of ideas…some great, some good, some bad. The concept is to unlock the creative part of your mind and let it roam free.

WHAT GREAT MORNING SHOWS SAY ABOUT SHOW PREP

Some of the industry's most respected morning pros on what makes good show prep:

• The best preparation is 8 hours sleep.

• Nothing's worse that flying by the seat of our pants. It's scary as hell!

• I try to be informed to the hilt, prepared, and that allows me to be confident and totally spontaneous. That sounds like a contradiction but it isn't. About 60% of my humor is ad-lib, top of mind zingers.

• For every hour on the air, prepare one hour off the air. By thinking ahead and making careful choices, you prepare your own "luck."

• As you read the morning paper, see if you can write a joke about each news story. You must train yourself to be funny.

• Reread the paper after your show. Go over it carefully and look for interesting information. You may never mention them on the air but it adds to your knowledge of the market.

- Eat a good breakfast. Be healthy.
- Exercising regularly is a tremendous boon to your general well being, especially if you get by on minimal sleep.
- Carry a hand-held recorder at all times. Just saying something into a recorder is easier than writing notes and it will come off more like it will on the air.

> **Talent Tip:**
> The last step in show prep is to go over your show "one more time" before hitting the air. It'll always "feel" different after you've slept on it.

IT'S A LOT OF WORK TO BE BRIEF

The longer it takes to get to the payoff, the greater the "price" your audience must pay.

$$Setup + Banter = Price$$
$$Payoff = Value$$

The less you "charge," the more they'll "buy." That is, the more they will listen!

Movies are made from books; both can take as long as they want to tell a story. But radio is a short-story format, and the #1 rule in writing short stories is to "begin as close to the end as possible, and work backwards."

Two of the most accomplished masters in history were Keats and Shelly. Included in their collection of letters to each other was one from Keats that began:

"I apologize for this letter. It will be long, for I don't have time to write a short one."

CHAPTER

8

CONCENTRATION

He was asked, "Why do you play so hard all the time — every day?"

He replied, "Because there may be someone in the stands that's never seen me play before."

"He" is the late, great Joe DiMaggio, perhaps the greatest Yankee ever.

T he next stage in putting your show on the air is probably the most difficult. It's the practice of concentration.

Concentration means focusing on what you are doing, and how listeners are receiving it. It means follow-through on the strategic plan, capitalizing on the hours of preparation. It's never being distracted from the goals you have set. Staying consistent, true to your personality.

Preparation without concentration is wasted. Concentration is a discipline that must be practiced. It's execution.

TAKING IT TO THE AIR

At this point, you have all your data. You know everything going on and have more information you can use. You have fun stuff, funny stuff, thought-provoking stuff, and controversial ideas too. Now what? How do great ideas get into a form that sounds real, natural, and creates a response?

> **Talent Tip:**
> *"Always swing hard, in case you actually hit the ball!"*
> *— Baseball great Duke Snider*

This is where we separate the men from the boys, the women from the girls, and the personalities from the DJs. When planning a show, lay it all out and brainstorm it in detail. Then, it's time to get creative. First, prioritize all the elements to be sure the most topical, relevant, and important information gets the most attention.

Go over all your material and determine if each element is:

• Timely in connection with someone in the news right now.

• An obvious connection.

For example, maybe there's a heavily promoted show on TV this week. Depending on if the show is good or bad, you may be able to use one of three bits that you brainstormed:

• What is the worst TV show you ever saw (or is on now)? Start with "Did you see _____ last night? What a bunch of nothing. It has to be the most disappointing new show of the season…and after all that hype. The last time I saw a show this bad was _____." Then, have a partner contribute another contender for bad shows, and set up a listener to talk about another. Presto, you're off and running.

- What is the funniest moment you ever saw on TV? Start with "Hey, you gotta check out _____, that new show that debuted this week. I mean, this is the first time in years I laughed out loud at a TV show. I think the last time that happened was _____ a few years ago. Now THAT was a funny show." That, same as above, will start the phone ringing!

The important thing is to realize the connection between your inspirations and the topical items you have. This doesn't have to be a direct, obvious match. In fact, many times the less obvious connection is more effective. Jeff & Jer are masters at taking something that happened in their experience and turning it "inside out," making it something that listeners take to a new level. You only have to find a creative connection that can be made to sound natural.

Exercise creative "linking" regularly and you'll soon discover that your problem is no longer "how do I get all this stuff on the air," but rather "how can I find the TIME to use all these great ideas?"

CREATING AN EMOTIONAL RESPONSE

Now that you understand the process of making a connection with the audience, let's take it up a notch. To be truly memorable and important, you have to create an *emotional* bond with your audience. The goal is to turn the information and preparation into something that connects with your audience. You must create a mood, an attitude. Your show must be constructed to provoke a reaction consistent with your personality goals. For example:

Laughter:	Give them a smile, a giggle, a laugh
Compassion:	Make them feel strongly about something
Joy:	Make them feel GOOD about something
Anger:	Get them stirred up, provoke a reaction

Patriotism: Make them proud of themselves and their community

Pride: Make them proud to be part of your show

Tradition: Family values, memories of the "old days"

Introspection: Did you know that...? Imagine what that feels like?

Each element should be targeted to address a specific emotion. And, many bits can be constructed to combine several emotional responses. For instance, if you "adopt" a family who has lost the father in an accident, you appeal to compassion (sympathetic responses), joy (feeling good about helping), tradition (family values), pride (make the listener feel good about helping), and introspection (puts them in the family's place).

Executed properly, this can be a very powerful thing. If two shows have the same idea simultaneously, the one who creates the emotional reaction and executes best will win. If another show hits on a great topic, but it's generic, *steal it*. With a personal, emotional spin on the same material, your show is the one listeners will be talking about.

You can take it away from them. But it takes planning, brainstorming, trouble-shooting, and follow through to make it pay off.

The "Who Cares" Test

Since the ultimate judge and jury of any show is the audience, remember that it doesn't matter how entertaining something is to you. It only matters what the audience thinks. Before anything goes on the air, you should make it pass the "who cares" test. Evaluate each idea, each bit, for who it will appeal to, how much and why. If it doesn't pass, it doesn't belong on the air.

Make Them Laugh, Make Them Cry

One of the things that make Jeff & Jer one of the world's premiere morning shows is their ability to create emotion in listeners. One day they have their listeners laughing hysterically with their one-liners and lightning wit. The next, they have them pulled off at the side of the road reapplying make up because the show has made them cry on the way to work.

Any show that creates a bond with listeners which sparks emotional responses will win the ratings war. Stir up feelings of anger, compassion, patriotism, lust, greed, fear, or any number of other possibilities. Identify an emotion, then create emotional moments on the radio and listeners can't turn off their radio because they're afraid of what they'll miss.

Great moments happen when personalities make that connection, as long as it's consistent with their core personality.

Jeff & Jer have one of the funniest shows on the planet. But humor is only one of the emotions they tap into. They're always alert to find a "warm fuzzy" that helps them develop more depth and dimension. And when they find it, they're smart enough to know how to go "over the top" and make an impact.

When a victim of domestic abuse called their show asking for help in a dangerous situation, Jeff & Jer didn't just refer her to an agency that could help. They became her friends, "adopting" her as a personal project. After a full show focused on the life and problems of "Becky," listeners took a personal stake in her future.

They made the audience care about the woman, then made it easy for listeners to get involved and help. Together, the station and listeners helped Becky start a new life. Then, at a time when many personalities would drop the topic, Jeff & Jer took it "over the top" by starting "Becky's Fund," which will build a shelter for dozens of women in similar situations.

Jeff & Jer exposed the horror of a problem that affects the lives of more people than most of us care to admit, and did it in a way that will further their image as being caring, sensitive, and in touch. It wasn't a wacky, outrageous, laugh-a-minute comedy gag as many elements on the show are. It was real. It was emotional. And it was *great* radio.

GETTING IT ON!

Just as Robert Redford and Paul Newman set up their victims in the classic "The Sting," personalities use several steps to making it work.

The "Hook"

"The Hook brings them back" — *Blues Traveler*

When you are ready to deliver your material, make sure you have set it up properly. Prepare your listener and "hook" them into the bit. You have to sell them the idea, the concept that you want them to respond to. You have to make it important to them. Give them a reason to care about what you are doing. That's not as simple as coming up with a clever name for your bit. You have to get to the heart of the matter, the hook!

Casey Casem is a master of the pre-sell. His classic benchmark is the "long distance dedication." But he never pre-sells that "a long distance dedication is coming up." Instead, he tells you a story that makes you want to hear more. He tells you that "a girl in Kansas writes about a high school relationship, broken up by family disaster, is back together through the magic of her ex-boyfriend's cocker spaniel Roy. That story and her song, coming up." He makes you want to hear more. He creates interest, and he does it with *specifics*. Not just a "dog" but a "cocker spaniel named Roy."

Brilliant pre-sell.

There is no standard length of time that a "hook," or pre-sell, or tease, should last. It depends on the bit. Some can be teased once or twice, others for an entire show. Some may last for several days or even a week. It depends on the payoff. There are even some examples of the hook lasting longer than the setup and payoff.

The Set-Up

After enticing your audience and stoking their interest, now you have to cultivate and nurture their involvement in the bit. This is where you give them a stake in your show. The setup requires that you provide sufficient information to the audience to make them understand what you are doing. In this step, it is important that you not assume they have heard the pre-sell. In fact, don't assume they know much at all. Explain the bit carefully, constantly resetting the stage. Be sure to build in some "hooks" along the way.

> *Talent Tip:*
> *The "set-up" may seem boring, but it's essential. It gives listeners the information they need to make sense out of the show. This is like the pass a guard makes to the center to execute the "alley-oop."*

Dress It Up

This is the time you make it sparkle. Use sound effects and appropriate listener reaction on the phones to help you develop the bit. Make everything you do entertaining. It's Show Biz! Be alert to opportunities to expand the bit during the setup/dress-up phase. A listener may suggest something that takes you to a new level. But don't lose focus on where you are going.

Instead of just reading something about Alanis Morissette, make it personal. "Hey, last week at the Alanis show, she told me right before she went on that…" Take credit!

Execution is everything. Don't become distracted. Concentration discipline requires that you focus on the facts and information. If you use listener interaction, be sure you coach them ahead of time. Set them up. Tell

Talent Tip:
Use personalization and
localization in the "dress
up" stage.

them what to say and help them know how to "perform" for you. This is critical if you want listener participation in your bit.

Like the pre-sell, the length of time for the set up will vary. Sometimes it can be far shorter than the pre-sell. Other times it may take longer to develop. With the Casey Casem example, this is the time he reads the letter from the girl in Kansas, letting her tell the story.

Also like the pre-sell, don't waste words. Wasted words cause boredom and diminish the impact. If there are wasted words, it's not well prepared. A great exercise is to start at the end, the payoff, and write "backwards," eliminating anything that is useless.

The Payoff

The payoff always comes last. Whether it's the punchline to a joke or the announcement of how much money you've raised for charity, this is the END. Be sure to build up, showcase the payoff and make it heard. Use production elements, staging, and drama to make it memorable.

This is also the stage to cash in your chips with the overwhelming emotional reaction. Whether it's what you're doing for a listener, or a laugh, make it count.

In our example, it's when Casey says "(name), this song is for you, a long distance dedication from the girl you thought you lost, now together again because of Roy." It makes you say "ah, how sweet."

The Blackout

It's critical to KNOW when the punchline is over, and to leave them with the emotional high. Take the listener to the emotional peak, then move on and let them experience it.

When the bit is over, it's OVER. Don't belabor it. Don't try to one-up what you've done. Like a comedian who goes for one too many punchlines, you can ruin a great bit by going too far in the payoff. End the party when everyone's having fun. Like George Castanza on "Seinfeld" says, "leave on a high note."

With any bit, the funnier, the bigger and more emotional the element, the farther you can go. But always leave the audience wanting a little bit more. A good rule of thumb is to never go for more than two punchlines. This gives you the element of surprise, or "over the top" but prevents you from confusing your audience or diluting the impact.

Casey's long distance dedication has a natural blackout when he plays the song. Sometimes he comes on after the song and backsells the bit, but usually just moves "on with the countdown."

Pre-Promotion

A major part of the concentration discipline is maintaining forward pace, momentum, and flow. This can be greatly enhanced with the application of pre-selling upcoming elements.

Why do we promote our upcoming features on the air? Simple. It's to motivate listeners to stay tuned and give us more quarter hours in their diary. Great. How can you get that wrong? A lot of jocks do.

Most air talent are doing a terrible job of selling the listener on listening longer. The programming staff may outwardly express a distaste for anything related to sales, but when it comes right down to it, everyone on the air is a salesperson. Everyone is representing his or her product to a consumer. Failure to effectively sell the benefits of your station results in lost sales.

Yet nearly every personality in America is just going through the motions with little enthusiasm or excitement when it comes to promoting the station.

When you construct any promotion, you must isolate the most important and compelling aspect of your announcement and answer the question, "What can I say about this that will cause my listener to want to hear more, react or participate?"

Here are some examples:

BAD: Hi, this is (your name here). I'll be with you until 3 o'clock this afternoon, then make way for (next jock).

BETTER: I'm (your name here). Just after 3 o'clock today, (next jock) will have another winner in the name-that-tune contest. I think you're next."

Be specific, be personal and explain exactly what is happening after the break

BAD: I'll be back in a minute with more music from Phil Collins, Color Me Badd and Mariah Carey.

BETTER: In the next 20 minutes, you'll hear that great new Mariah Carey record, along with a Phil Collins classic from 1984 — remember "Against All Odds?" I have that for you too.

Again, promote specifically and sell the upcoming elements instead of just reading a laundry list of artists coming up. Highlight key benefits and even play a quick music hook of potentially unfamiliar songs or artists. Oh, and get away from the phrase "I'll be back"...where are you going?

BAD: Coming up, we'll have a check on weather, sports, and more winners.

BETTER: The new weather forecast is out, and it looks great for your weekend plans...I'll have that, along with another chance to win concert tickets for Thursday night's (artist) show at the auditorium, next.

BAD: Another Candid Phone call, the word of the day and much more coming up on the morning zoo.

BETTER: At 7:25, we have another candid phone call...this one is to an exterminator in (town) that (premise of call)...it's hilarious, and it's coming up on WXXX.

Promotion means selling. Provide relatables that really mean something to the listener. Give them a chance to WANT to listen to what you have planned.

MODERATION

"If you don't do it excellently, don't do it at all.
Because if it's not excellent, it won't be profitable
or fun, and if you're not in business for fun or
profit, what are you doing there?"

— Robert Townsend, author of Up The
Organization and former CEO of Avis

oderation can be the most difficult discipline to master. It's knowing "when to say 'when'."

It's natural to get carried away when the show is on a roll, and lose perspective on the listener's point of view. Many shows do everything exceptionally well, but have no sense of when to "turn it off and move on."

Moderation also means balance. It's the art of providing diverse, consistent entertainment elements that expand the appeal of the show. The amazing demographic attraction of great morning shows is achieved in part because of this balance.

There's no set of "rules" or principles to help guide shows in the practice of moderation. It's a feeling, a sense of control. It develops over time and is in a constant state of evolution. It's a difficult, subjective discipline, and it's key to making the show work.

Often, the difficult task of monitoring the show and keeping it on track falls in the lap of the producer. He or she is in a position to hear the show more objectively, and offer feedback that can provide insight.

THE COST OF LISTENING!

Why is moderation so important? Consider it cost control. Many broadcasters engage in long philosophical discussions about the challenge of developing avid, passionate core listeners. After all, they argue, radio is free and listeners don't appreciate the value of radio.

It's true that listeners don't actually *pay* to listen, but there is a cost of listening to the radio. Consider your station, or your show, to be a retail shop. When listeners (shoppers) come to your frequency (store), they seek to hear (purchase) something very specific. It could be to hear their favorite song, get into a particular mood, be entertained by the personalities, or win a contest.

The longer it takes your listener (customer) to find what he or she wants, the higher the cost of the listening experience. Too many commercials? The cost goes up. Mindless chatter, without any direction or payoff? It gets more costly. A contest that doesn't relate to the listener? It's getting expensive! When the cost gets too high, the listener punches the button (shops somewhere else).

Yes, they'll probably be back. But if they begin finding the same (or heaven forbid, *better*) products elsewhere at a lower *cost*, eventually they'll think of your competitor as their new "favorite store."

Many people would rather buy tools from a hardware store than a discount department store, even if they pay 20% more. They know the item will be in stock, it'll be easy to find, and they'll save time. Many listeners today are also going to specialty shops with their listening "dollars."

Are you making it difficult for your listener to shop at your store? Exercise moderation, focus your product, and honestly evaluate your performance through the ears of your listener and you will have a much better chance of maintaining low prices, great service, and loyal customers!

DISCERNING PROPER MODERATION

The most difficult part of the concept of moderation is that it is so subjective. It's vague, difficult to measure, and open to vast differences in interpretation.

The telltale signs that moderation may be an issue include:

1. Slow pace or tempo
2. Great material but the payoff disappoints
3. Great bits but the overall show doesn't sparkle
4. Steady diet of material that appeals to same emotions

You've probably heard many shows that "sound great" when you break down all the bits, all the elements. It's hard to criticize. On paper, it's terrific. But on the air, it somehow leaves you unexcited. When you hear a show like this, it's probably a problem with moderation. The section on Evaluating the Show will help with this principle.

SECTION

3

COMEDY

"Comedy Is Not Pretty"

— Steve Martin

Most air personalities make the mistake of believing that the most important part of any show is humor. Day after day, hour after hour, they strive to be funny. When their attempts at making the audience laugh fall short, they try harder and agonize for one-liners that make them feel like they are truly funny.

In case you haven't noticed, there are very few genuinely funny air personalities. Letterman has a team of writers that work all day long to come up with his material, and he's not on for four hours a day!

There's no substitute for a funny morning show. The ability to make people laugh is a special talent. Those that have it have a tremendous advantage. But, being funny is not all-important.

The ability to identify what is funny and mold it into a form that meshes with an overall personality is far more significant in the success of a radio show. There are many ways to get a smile, a giggle or a laugh, if you know how to use them. Remember, it's creating a mood that makes a show successful.

MAKING
IT
FUNNY

omedy is all around you. Most of the great humorists rely on simply pointing out things that are already there. You don't need to reinvent things. Delivery is the most important. Humor on a show is great if it's done properly, and consistently. Make sure the audience knows how to take you, what to expect. Your "punchlines" should be the surprise.

The single most important thing any aspiring writer (or personality) must learn is structure. Put the show in the proper context. The funniest part of Letterman each night is the Top 10 list. Not because it's actually the funniest thing, but because of the expectation he has built up through consistency. It's in the proper structure and context. We know what to expect.

After developing a comedy style, or expectation, stick with the formula. Don't alter it. Remember "New Coke"? Don't mess with success.

As funny bits are developed, keep in mind the point of view of the personality. The payoff has to be consistent with what the audience would expect from the talent. Howard Stern doing Rick Dees' material wouldn't sound right, or be very funny, would it?

WHEN IN DOUBT, CUT IT OUT

Most comedy comes from asking "what if" in the brainstorming sessions. "What if" leads to wild, free wheeling ideas and it's amazing what can emerge. Most writers end up with far more than they can ever use. The rule of thumb is to edit anything marginal. There is no place in radio humor for attempts at comedy that fail to hit the mark.

Be objective. Edit. Less is more. Anything that doesn't add to the humor detracts from it. Above all, be willing to murder your darlings. Know when to bail out. Be objective. It's probably not nearly as funny as you think it is.

In most shows, comedy is likely to be involved somehow in the recipe.

Brainstorming Comedy

A good method for writing comedy material is simple brainstorming sessions. Use all members of the show and staff. Start with a list of all the major headlines. From that list, make a second one that contains word associations relating to each topic, issue, or person in column 1. Then, lump words and thoughts together to create funny thoughts that become bits.

Here's an example from several years ago:

• Two unrelated headlines:
   A. Bert Parks is fired as host of the Miss America Pageant for drinking
   B. Northwest Airlines admits two pilots were legally drunk when they flew a plane from Minneapolis to Detroit.

• Creative Spark: Put the two unrelated stories together and get this: The Miss America Pageant fired Bert Parks as host today, citing his drinking problem. He should be okay though. According to his agent, he's taken a job as pilot for Northwest Airlines.

TYPES
OF
COMEDY

*There are many forms of humor. Identifying them
will help in the selection process of what fits a show.
WARNING: JOKES are hard to tell on the air. To
make any joke work, it MUST be re-worked into
the normal flow of the show.*

Blue Humor

It's really not that hard to be funny on the air. There is a common thread that runs through everyone's sense of humor — sex! Almost everyone can be funny with this topic, but it's another thing to be successful using it. Howard Stern makes it work for him. But relying on the "lowest common denominator" to drive the humor of a show is only successful for a few. It doesn't take much talent to tell dirty jokes. It DOES take talent to tiptoe up to that imaginary line, paint a picture with words, and finesse a punchline so it stays fresh and interesting.

One way to get away with blue humor on the air is to let the audience do your dirty work. Lay it out there and let them draw the conclusions. Take the audience to the scene of the crime, place the weapon in their hands and let them deliver the fatal blow. For example:

- A character on your show (caller) calls and tells you the joke or throws out the one-liner that you would like to deliver. You, of course, express shock and dismay that anyone would say this on your show.
- One of the members of the show takes on a "bad boy" personality by being the one that always goes "over the line." The rest of the show chastises him for being that way.
- Creatively set up "Seinfeld" type discussions where you talk around the subject without referring to it directly ("Master of My Domain").
- Do a "Dirty Joke of the Day" where the joke's setup is given at 7 am, and the punchline half an hour later. Both are totally innocent by themselves. It also creates longer TSL.

Blue humor is not the most creative way to get a laugh, but it works. The key is to make it work within the context of the personality of the show.

Exaggeration

Exaggeration is a simple concept that is very effective. It's also easy to get listeners to help if you get them started. Here are a few examples:

- Millie, the White House Dog, is so smart, that when she was being paper trained, she learned to read.

- My hometown is so small, that when my girl friend plugged in her vibrator, the streetlights dimmed.
- Two men were walking through hell when a blast of cold air hit them. Soon it started snowing. As the snow got deeper and deeper, one turned to the other and said 'Huh, the Cubs must have won the World Series."

Even talent that is not naturally funny can come up with some exaggeration lines for most any relevant topic. It's probably part of their everyday life already. When brainstorming comedy material using exaggeration, overstate your purpose. Nothing is too extreme, too outrageous, or too farfetched.

Once you have a page of ideas on a topic, start working on verbiage and narrow the focus. This is one of the most common types of comedy in everyday life. Just adapt it to the radio!

Moron Jokes Revisited

The great thing about moron jokes is that they can be revised and reworked to fit many current situations. In a way, they are timeless. It just takes a little effort. For example:

- Can you believe what (local celebrity) just did? (Discuss topic.) He's the kind of guy that would take up nude painting and get pneumonia.
- (Politician) is just not very bright. (discuss topic). In college, he worked at a bank and they caught him stealing pens.

Naivete

Naivete works for many personalities as a tool of comedy development. Not that the goal of a personality should be for the audience to perceive them as a buffoon, but being the victim of occasionally being naive will make them endearing forever. Everyone loves an underdog. Everyone relates to someone who reveals vulnerabilities.

As a comedic tool, use naive jokes as part of a personality, not as the main part of a personality. Be sure to work them in carefully to fit in the proper context. Examples:

- (In discussing the difference in kids now and when they went to school): I went to school in a different time. In fact, until I was a junior in college, I thought intercourse was the break between classes.
- Then there's the old joke of "how can I be overdrawn when I have so many checks left."

Mundane Aspects Of A Big Event

Everybody talks about the big events. The challenge is figuring out how to break them down and be unique and different. Talk about things that matter to your audience, but not the obvious things everyone else will rehash.

Brainstorm big events in detail and break it down until you come up with something useful:

- The Jerry Lewis telethon was so dull, they gave half the money to yawn research.

Phony Survey/Statistics

There are surveys and statistics for everything! And most are a bit waiting to happen. Just open any of the women's magazines and a week's worth of material awaits. A couple of ways to use surveys:

- Use the information, then add a punchline. Have you seen the new Cosmo? They claim that 71% of single females would not make love on the first date (true). My question is, "Where can I get the numbers of the other 29%?"
- Go through the survey, then add a (your show) survey of your own, kind of like Letterman's Top 10 list.

Unrelated Items Forced Together

This is one of the easiest ways to be funny, after you get the hang of it. Make a list of what is going on in the world today. Headlines only. Then, add a punchline by putting two unrelated elements together. It's easy. You'll have more one liners than you can use and it's very topical. Example:

- Safe Sex and Airline Safety: United is taking airline safety a little too far. The last flight I was on, the safety demo included how to wear a condom. Let's see, insert here, and pull tight across your lap…OUCH.

Intentional Misunderstanding

The basis for thousands of jokes you've heard and told, it's easy to work into jokes but difficult to make it work on the air.

- Did you hear the name of the new Ronald Reagan movie? Partial Recall.
- A man walks up to a second man with a dog sitting next to him. He asks "Does your dog bite?" "No," said the second man. The first man reaches down to pet the dog but the dog takes a big chunk right out of him. "Hey, I thought you said your dog didn't bite." The other guy says, "He doesn't. That's not my dog."

Good News/Bad News

This takes more effort but it can be worthwhile.

- The good news is I got a hole in one on the sixth hole. Bad news is we were playing the fifth.
- So, I'm on the phone waiting to get the report from my doctor, and the nurse comes on and says, "I've got good news Mrs. White." "It's MISS White," I say. "Oh, in that case, I have bad news."

This is another fairly simple form of comedy to execute. It just takes time playing the "what if" game and brainstorming.

Facts Stated

This is also easy to work into a show if it fits into one of the show's characters, or a regular caller that is "known" by the listeners. Take two unrelated facts and put them together to produce something absurd. The right type of show can make this a great kicker to a newscast.

- The Kinsey Institute says 60% of men and women know that the average size of a man's erect penis is 5 to 7 inches. Sounds like a prison sentence…5-7 with a chance for early release.

This is a very difficult comedy form to master. Most personalities that attempt this type of "wisecrack" humor often sounds corny or forced. If it works, it can be terrific. If not, it's deadly.

Pushing Logic Past Reality

While it first appears that this is similar to exaggeration, it has slightly different characteristics. Take a topic, and extend it to an illogical or absurd extreme of something real. Ask yourself, "If this happened, then what?" This can work on almost any show. It just takes brainstorming time to ask "What if?"

- Things have changed with women and their status in society. 20 years ago it was men asking women about measurements. Now it's women asking men about theirs. I say, "Thank God for the metric system."
- It's just dropped 10 degrees in the last hour. If this keeps up tomorrow morning we'll all have freezer burn.
- A man was sued for divorce on the grounds of being sterile. At the same time, his secretary filed a paternity suit against him. The weird thing is, he lost both cases.

Observational Questions

This is also pretty easy if time is taken to brainstorm the punchline. Find something absurd, add a punchline and presto! "Does that mean…" Jerry Seinfeld has made a career out of this, as has Steven Wright.

- Why is it that every time you wash clothes, you end up with one odd sock? Where do all these socks go? Does this mean there's some kind of sock limbo, or a sock purgatory for bad socks with holes in them?

What If

Again, be curious, inquisitive and brainstorm.

- What if Yoko Ono married Mario Cuomo after a failed marriage to

Sonny Bono? Would she be Yoko Ono Bono Cuomo?

This takes a bit more creativity and original thought than other forms of comedy. It also has the potential of missing the mark because it can be "off-topic."

Switch

Take a real element on the top of people's minds. Then take out a key part of the story and replace it.

- At the recent AMA Convention, a doctor broke a bone in his back when he sat on a chair and broke it. As he tumbled to the ground, another doctor screamed, "Is there a carpenter in the house?"
- The Attorney General is not in. Would you care to leave your fingerprints?

Applying "switch" to your show can be very effective, but takes a lot of time to develop.

Old Joke/New Twist

Take a classic joke and update it. Perfect for old blonde jokes or redneck jokes. Pick out one area of the market and pick on it. Be sure someone from the show is from that area so they can defend it, softening the impact.

- How many (people from suburb) does it take to make chocolate chip cookies? 10. One to make the batter and 9 to peel the M & Ms.

Anachronism

Take those old, dumb jokes and set them up to relate to the audience.

- First person: I can't believe the luck I had at a garage sale on (street) this weekend. I got a VCR that belonged to Lyndon Johnson, the president. Second person: The VCR wasn't invented until the 70s. Johnson was president in the 60s. First person: I guess that's what makes this so rare.

SECTION

4

EVALUATING THE SHOW

I n a perfect world, air talent would receive regular, constructive, positive feedback. The PD would be supportive, upbeat, and consistent in all dealings. He or she would shield talent from the GM and sales department and run interference from other departments. The PD would be the talent's biggest fan and establish credibility so any criticism is respected.

But this is reality, not fantasyland. Most talent is starved for attention and feedback of any kind. They are left alone to make the show and station as great as it can be. Not getting input, or getting bad input is not an excuse for lack of improvement.

Great morning shows have an ability to step back and be objective. They have the discipline of hearing the show through the ears of the audience. They seek input from those they respect and force them to be honest in their criticism. Remember, evaluating a show isn't an exercise to stroke an ego. It's to make the talent great. To be great, you have to find out how to improve. Improvement only comes with a hungry, humble spirit.

Every member of the show should be involved in the evaluation process. It should start with the PD, of course. And, everyone must take a sacred vow to be honest.

For the PD, it's even more complex. How do you know if your current show has potential? Is the show "maxed out" or has it just reached a temporary plateau? Are they going through the usual growing pains, or is the show destined to be "ordinary?" If it's ordinary, how do you keep them motivated and send the message they can't talk more? How do you push them to do more, while trying to limit them in some areas? These are some of the most difficult questions you will ever have to address.

Evaluating and recognizing whether the show is "on" is difficult. The success of a bit or show is very subjective and there is generally a lot of disagreement about what works. To measure progress, you need a set of objective criteria that can be applied regularly. To evaluate a morning show, you have to *listen*. A lot. Closely. Keep detailed notes on everything. See the sample monitor forms in this chapter for an example on how to keep track of how a show is really hitting the mark.

CHAPTER

12

GRADING
THE
SHOW

onsultant Randy Lane has developed a comprehensive list of 23 areas to grade shows:

Role Definition: Are the participants on the show staying within the role that they fill? Is character development consistent? Is everyone participating in the way their role was originally conceived? Does every role "make sense"?

Attitude/Style: What is the mood, the feeling that comes from the show? Is it fulfilling your goals? Does it sound like the image you set out to portray? Is it consistent from day to day, hour to hour, break to break?

Synchronicity: Does the show make sense? Is everything coming together to be greater than the sum of its parts? Or are there bits and elements that come from out of "left field" and don't really connect? Do listeners "get it?"

Planning: How is the show prep process working? Is everyone prepared and doing what it takes to be great? Do you know what's happening locally? Nationally? On TV? In the movies? Sports? Does everyone know what is going to happen every day before it happens? Is the daily road map working? What do we need? Is anyone beating us on topicality? Why?

Localization: Does the show sound like your market, or could you plop it down anywhere in the country with equal success? Are you mentioning neighborhoods, streets, landmarks, and suburbs? Do you talk in the language and style of the locals? Are you telling "stories"?

Listener Involvement: Are they participating with the show consistently? Is your material designed to make it easy for them to interact? Is it "user friendly"? Do you save the best part of phone calls for re-use? Do you have a bank of "ringers" ready to contribute whenever they're needed?

Consistency: Do listeners know what to expect? Is each portion of the show a snapshot of the entire show? Do you deliver all the elements of your show regularly? Are there benchmarks that help listeners "reconstruct" their listening?

Structure: Does the show "flow" well? Is there a road map that guides you from one element to the next? Even Picasso had structure…the canvas on which he painted.

Vocal Dynamics/Quality: Are you projecting properly? Getting the most out of your voice? Is there too much laughter or giggling? Is the laughter appropriate? Is there enough laughter? Do we sound confident? Tentative? Nervous? Shy?

Humor/Entertainment: You don't have to give them a punchline or belly laugh each time but there should at least be a smile or good feeling. Does the show have a sense of humor? Is it consistent? Does the humor fit into the image you want to project? Is the type of humor in line with the mission statement?

Bit Construction: Is the show well thought out? Have you planned on how to get into and out of the bit? How could you have brainstormed it better? Weak bits can become memorable with the right set up and presentation. Conversely, great bits are flat if they are properly executed. Do you tend to "rip and read" too much?

Spontaneity: Planned or unplanned, do you give the listener some surprises within the framework of the show? Is there an "oh wow" factor? Does it sound fun, freewheeling and natural or stiff, planned, and scripted? You should never tip your hand in the spirit of being "real." It's not only okay to surprise the audience, it's your duty. Do things that are unexpected (within role definition).

Production Values: Are there proper sound effects, music beds, drops, etc.? Are phone calls and snippets used properly? More importantly, is the show over produced? Don't let it sound like a zoo...that's OUT. Does the production accent and highlight the bit or does it detract by being too overbearing?

Creativity: Is the show fresh, progressive, and original? Are you putting fresh spins on old ideas (or stolen ideas)? Or are you just reading USA Today? Do you introduce new benchmarks and retire old ones when they've run their course?

Topicality: Are you talking about the things that interest your target or are you boring them with things they don't care about? Are you missing any big stories? Are you giving enough attention to what is really on top of people's minds? The normal tendency is to drop a topic quickly because "we already did something with that" when the listener is still buzzing about it. Are you truly plugged into the lifestyle of your listener?

Communication Skills: Are you relating and communicating naturally to your audience or are you "announcing?" Are you putting your thoughts into the language and verbiage your audience uses or do you sound like a "broadcaster?" Are you a real person that they would like to know or a distant, lifeless DJ? Do you really LISTEN to your callers or just jam your thoughts on the air?

Information: Are you getting the service elements everyone needs? Time, temp, weather, traffic, news, sports? Are you delivering the audience expectation clearly, and in a consistent, timely fashion? Do you promote the station? Are you relating to the music and selling the songs and artists? Do you sell the benefits of the station and your own show?

Fundamentals: Are you promoting upcoming bits properly? Does the show have good pace and forward momentum? Are you brief enough? Do you constantly reset the stage to include your audience so they know what you are doing?

Realness: Does the show sound like real people, or is there an element of "phoniness" in it? Are you sincere? Natural? Relatable? Or does it sound put on, like you're trying too hard? Does it sound like a "DJ" or a real person?

Specialty: Are you delivering the "specialness" that makes your show unique? Is the character of the show different from all your competitors? Does it stand out? What did you/are you delivering that nobody else in your market can do?

It's a great list, but here are a couple more dimensions:

Emotion: Are they looking for the emotional angle? Not every hour, or even every morning, but at least regularly?

Imagination: Are they looking for interesting ways to deal with topics and events? Is the show constantly looking for ways to make people talk?

Ambition: Is the show's idea of being creative just "giving something away"? Are they working hard, or just going through the motions?

PERSONALITY PERFORMANCE MEASUREMENT	Possible Points	Your Figure
1. ON-AIR PERFORMANCE (Total 100)		
A. *Time Clock Orientation* - how well do you relate to what listeners are thinking, feeling, and doing?	10	
B. *Attitude/Vibe* - Have you picked them up and made them feel good?	10	
C. *Emotion/Passion* - Have you tugged their heartstrings? Do you have passion for the music? Do you sound like you really are playing great classics/the best new songs?	10	
D. *Topicality/Localism/Information* - Listeners expect you to be the service for information that is relevant to their lives, tailored to their lifestyles and tuned into their needs, what's going on now or later, what's coming up this week.	10	
E. *Compelling* - your creative hooks and teases are so good, listeners can't turn off, because they're afraid they will miss something.	10	
F. *Formatic Discipline* - Attaching station to music intros, back sells and station information features. How much credit did the station get? How well are you packaging the elements?	10	
G. *Audience Interaction* - On air phone calls, Reaction Line - is it entertaining? Word economy.	10	
H. *Show Prep/Quotability* - What really interesting pieces did you bring to the show? Seize the moment opportunities - surfing the city's wave. Was it entertaining?	10	
I. *Cross Promotion of Other Personalities* - Give them compelling reasons to listen to other dayparts on the station.	10	
J. *Overall Level of Entertainment* - After sampling your show today, would listeners forsake another station to listen to your show tomorrow? Uniqueness.	10	

Tracy Johnson & Alan Burns

2. HOUSEKEEPING	60	
A. On Air maintenance, ensuring all promos, liners are played and signed off.		
B. Effort in finding missing material.		
C. Studio cleanliness and work areas tidiness		
D. Alerting Engineers to Problems		

3. OFF AIR COMMITMENT		
A. Listener Contact	60	
• Answering listener correspondence		
• Phone attitude		
• Answering the phone after hours and on weekends		
• Handling listener inquiries		
• Answering critics and listener letters		
B. Promotions	60	
• General availability		
• Prize delivery		
• Ideas		
• Attending station promotional activities		
• Wearing station gear		
C. Production	60	
• Creative input into production (movie bits, sweepers, promo angles)		
• Creative input into copy and promos		
• Availability for production		
• Taking direction		
D. Attitude	50	
• Willingness to pitch in, take and maintain direction		
• Create good station morale, your attitude towards work colleagues		
E. Meeting Attendance	60	
• Announcers		
• Promotions		
• Training		
• Staff		
• Brainstorming		
4. SALES	60	
A. Sales referral		
B. Visiting clients with Reps		
C. Attending client functions		
D. Attending client brainstorming sessions		

CHAPTER 13

THE MORNING SHOW MEETING

Of course everyone hates meetings. The most valuable lesson I've learned about going to meetings is that most meetings are not needed. But the morning show meeting is different. It's not fun, but you *Gotta* do it! Daily. It's one of the little things that makes the difference between doing well and winning!

Skipping the meetings is often a sign of laziness, and that leads to failure. It implies that you are satisfied with the show just the way it is, and that's never acceptable. It's okay to be happy with a show, but not satisfied. Tomorrow's show must be better. Don't coast. Be driven by the art of your craft. What is acceptable today is a loser tomorrow. When you stop changing, you stop growing.

Depending on your organization and structure, your meeting may take on many forms, and no two meetings will be the same. If they are the same, they become routine. Routine is redundant. Redundant is boring. Boring is bad.

The morning show meeting can be productive and exhilarating or the most dreaded part of the day. Not having meetings is deadly. So is having one that doesn't make you better.

Most meetings won't require a lot of formality but do require some structure. Make it fun, and don't belabor small, insignificant points. Keep it upbeat. The entire show should be present, and everyone should be required to contribute. The PD should be involved most, if not all, of the time. As the show matures, the PD's involvement can be reduced, but should never disappear.

Change the meeting place from time to time. Get out of the office. Do lunch. Break up the monotony. Somebody (probably the producer) should take accurate, detailed notes and provide needed follow-up. And no outsiders are allowed. No guests, unless agreed upon by the team.

No egos are allowed. This is an open session that is to make everyone better. No politics, no agenda. Anyone can say anything in this meeting. It's all one TEAM.

Meetings should be conducted with passion and compassion. Keep it positive and let everyone know you're all working together. Keep meetings short, but don't leave anything out. It's too important. Make the meeting fast paced.

Major Areas Of Focus:

1. Schedule all meetings immediately following the show, while it's fresh in everyone's mind. Also, it removes all excuses for not attending. It's like making children do their homework right after school, before they watch TV or play with their friends.

2. Hold all calls. NO interruptions. Make it the most important part of everyone's day. If talent is going to consider the meeting important, it has to be important to the PD.

3. Review the show, either mentally or physically (using an aircheck). Talk about what was good, and bad, and why.

4. Emphasize good breaks. Build on the positive.

5. Examine breaks that could be better. Did we miss any opportunities by not exploring some angles? Should we have ended the break earlier? It's like a golfer analyzing his swing after the tournament. The *result* is less important than the mechanics in this meeting.

6. Map/plan tomorrow's show. Brainstorming/idea time! This is usually the fun part of the meeting.

7. Review the next day's content. How will we approach topics tomorrow? How can we put together a show that is memorable?

8. Discuss future shows/promotions/ideas. Long term planning. How can we get involved to make the show better?

9. General discussion. Any problems? Never let personal issues go unresolved. Many successful marriages have a simple rule of "never going to bed angry"…you should never leave the station with any problems looming.

MAKING MEETINGS WORK

Well-intended meetings often go astray as your day fills up. Not only that, effective meetings are not always easy to implement. There's a tendency to get hung up on unimportant details, or certain members of the show are reluctant to contribute. If you're having a hard time making good use of your time, here's an outline you can use to start:

1. What worked well today? Why? What made it work? How could it have been better? Should we do this bit again? When? How often? How could/should it be modified next time? What one thing did we do that made it memorable?

2. What didn't go well today? Why? If we repackaged it or approached it differently, could it have worked? Should we try it again? When? What will make it better next time?

3. What did we have planned that we had no time for today? Should we lose it, or try to fit it in tomorrow? Is it still relevant?

4. What is happening in our community? In the market? At the station? What are our competitors doing?

5. How can we address these events tomorrow? How can we localize to touch our listeners? Can we work these events into already established features or benchmarks, or do they have to stand on their own?

6. What is topical today? What is your target listener thinking? What are they talking about? What are their concerns? What makes them angry? What is making them laugh? What are they doing tonight? Tomorrow? This weekend?

7. Each person should take a turn relating what they did last night or are planning to do soon. It must relate to the target.

8. What is a good phone topic for tomorrow? How can we get into it easily and naturally?

9. What other ways can we involve listeners in our show?

10. What issues are being talked about in specific neighborhoods around town?

11. What personality or character can we call for a perspective on an issue or topic?

12. What signature features or benchmarks should we use tomorrow?

13. Who is in town, or coming to town soon? Concerts, or other events. Can we get them on or involve them somehow?

14. Who can we call for interesting, weird, outrageous, or humorous conversation? Or are there relevant celebrities we can call and have on tomorrow?

15. What are we doing tomorrow that will evoke emotion in a listener? Emotion of any kind!

16. What production values can we add to the show? Clips from TV, videos, movies, song parodies, music beds, breakers, production effects, etc.

17. What information bits should we consider adding? How would we position it?

18. What events, holidays or occasions are coming up? Start planning NOW for the future.

19. What games and contests are we doing tomorrow? What are the prizes? What's more important tomorrow...the prize or the game?

20. What is the most memorable thing about tomorrow's show? How can we create talk in the marketplace tomorrow.

START WITH THE BASICS

Every show should establish a routine to quickly review each element from the show, either formally or informally. Many days will be quick, but you should break down an entire show regularly. Don't be too "hard" on an off day, and don't heap excessive praise on a "good" show. Be objective and work toward improving every day.

Each "bit" should be rated:

• IT WORKED. Do it again — soon!

• It was okay. Modify it and try again. But, brainstorm HOW to modify it.

• IT SUCKED. Never again!

Solve disagreements between participants by referring to the aircheck for that day's show. Sometimes you may think something "sucked" but it could have worked if it were repackaged. Listening to an aircheck can be useful.

> **Talent Tip:**
> **Nothing will ever be**
> **attempted if all possible**
> **objections must be**
> **overcome.***

Most importantly, someone must be in charge. While you want general agreement on what works and what doesn't, it's not a democracy. Somebody has to take responsibility for breaking the "ties." After all, even if everyone in the meeting votes for a dumb idea, it's still a dumb idea.

THE DREADED AIRCHECK

For the most part, try to avoid aircheck review sessions. Nobody likes going over the tape in detail. However, you should regularly use airchecks as part of the process. It's especially helpful in focusing on the areas often ignored.

Most talent hate listening to airchecks. If your morning talent is a sports fan, try this analogy: Can you imagine a football team NOT reviewing film of a game? The team that doesn't study what works well, and what broke down, usually gets a high draft choice, because they don't win many games. Going over airchecks is the radio equivalent of football teams watching the game film.

The daily evaluation can be as part of an aircheck, but doesn't have to be. Airchecks are usually misused. Going through every grueling moment of a show can be a gigantic waste of time. After all, everyone knows when a bit didn't work, and when something could have been done to make it better, right? But there are times when an aircheck session is appropriate, and listening regularly is essential in the process of striving for greatness.

There are at least three great ways to use airchecks, and both have their advantages:

1. **The skimmer:** Listen carefully to everything you say and how you say it. Tear it apart in detail. Be brutal, merciless. Pay attention to the details. Don't try this often. It's tedious, fatiguing and can be demoralizing to talent.

2. **The "real time" aircheck:** Record the entire show on cassette…don't edit anything. Then, listen to the show on Saturday or Sunday morning so you can hear the show the way a listener does, in real time. Get their perspective on your show while you go about your business. It will open your eyes to a whole new way of approaching your show.

3. **Selective aircheck:** Talk about specific improvements in technique or presentation. Then listen to the aircheck specifically for examples of the topic at hand. This is usually very effective and is accepted as much more positive.

Evaluating a show via aircheck is a tedious, time consuming procedure. Many morning shows become lazy and can't figure out why they're slipping, but when they examine their performance closely they find that they have been talking more than usual, and not following through on the basics. The aircheck is the only way to bring it back to center.

Skimmer Tape Tips

To help evaluate the basics, here are some things to listen for when going over a skimmer aircheck:

- **Shorten Intros.** Examine wording and phrasing. Shorten to a bare minimum for absolute clarity. Complex intros lead to clutter and tune out. Make sure teases and setups are not "DJ terms," but are communicated the way listeners talk. Be concise, and tight. Long breaks that ramble are a sign of laziness.

- **Make Contests Listener Oriented.** In fact, make the whole SHOW listener oriented. Are your contests quick? Easy to play? Easy to understand? Entertaining to non-players? Do produced elements enhance the bit, or compete with it?

- **Promote the Station First.** Every time. This is NOT YOUR SHOW. It's the station's show. Promote the station, positioning statement, and other aspects or dayparts as appropriate. Sell it! There aren't many winning morning shows on losing radio stations.

- **Presell Upcoming Bits Constantly.** Every 10-15 minutes. Get them to tune in frequently or listen a bit longer, and you will win. Tell them what you're going to do! The show should constantly move forward. When one segment winds down, the next should be pre-sold with an effective billboard "hook" to keep the anticipation high.

- **Localize.** Personalize it for your audience. Instead of "I read about it in the paper…" say "Judy from (area) called this morning and told me about…" Use local landmarks, suburbs, streets, etc. If you want to relate to your audience, you have to know your market. Never let them forget that you live here, too. Make local experience the fabric of the show.

TOP 10 TALENT TROUBLES

The biggest problem between air talent and programmers is usually the most fundamental. The basics. Just like major league baseball teams constantly emphasize proper baserunning and bunt coverage, talent should regularly work on their fundamentals.

Most problem areas are simple matters that should be (and usually are) taken for granted. Talent doesn't think about them any more. They've heard it all before. They know what they do wrong, but no longer are sensitive to mistakes when they occur. Here are the 10 most common fundamentals that shows need to constantly work on:

1. **Lack of preparation.** Opening the mike without a clear direction or knowing exactly what is going to happen next. The result is a slow pace, pointless talk and chatter that contributes nothing.

2. **Content that is hard to understand.** This is usually a result of not being prepared. The material is fine, but the communication skills needed to deliver the bit were weak. The solution is simple analysis of the structure of the break to remind talent that simple is best!

3. **Multiple thought sets.** Random subject changes. No setup, or payoff to a bit. Eliminate small talk (another sign of being unprepared). Don't be generic. Remember, it's better to go deeper into fewer subjects than have too many topics going on at once.

4. **Emphasis on the wrong material.** Irrelevant information, lack of understanding about what is important or entertaining. It's easy to get caught up in what we're doing and lose focus on what is important to the listener.

5. **Lack of immediacy.** The big advantage of radio over all other media is that it is versatile. Make it happen now.

6. **Lack of station identification.** Promoting the show over the station, or not promoting the station with enthusiasm or excitement.

7. **Lack of content.** Laziness, not working to find something new to relate to. Going through the motions without preparing.

8. **Leaning on cliches or crutches.** Bad habits are easy to fall into. What are they doing to get out of them? Part of the evaluation

process should be to raise awareness of possible irritating habits you might miss otherwise.

9. **Incorrect formatic placement of elements.** This is carelessness or disregard for station policies and good formatics.

10. **Complicating something simple.** Again, bad execution and communication skills.

PD CONDUCT

Part of any leader's job is to raise self-esteem and confidence of individual members of the team. If people feel good about themselves, they perform better. The PD's responsibility in all dealings with talent is to establish self-confidence, which will push the performer to greater heights.

> **Talent Tip:**
> **Great PDs constantly push the talent to greater heights with fresh ideas and thought stimulation.**

A leader will also give up power to become stronger. He or she will listen more than speak. Strive to gain trust and build a relationship with the talent.

Winning PDs always take a positive approach...all day, every day. Upbeat thinking is central to winning, and building self-confidence in the team. Positive thinkers achieve positive results.

The goals should always be constant improvement. Every day. Every show. Progress toward the goal. It will come in stages. There's a difference between being "great" and being "just a talent." Talented people reach quotas but do nothing to make the organization better. Great performers raise their own level of performance and that of their co-workers. To be truly great requires constant improvement. It challenges those around them. Most people don't want to work that hard. Find those that do, and inspire them!

MORNING SHOW "MONITOR"

When you monitor a morning show for later evaluation, it's a good idea to write everything down. Here's an example of a very useful monitor. Use it in the evaluation process regularly…and keep every written monitor. It helps to compare how the show sounds NOW with how it has sounded in the past!

Note how the personal notes and comments go under each element…good for remembering the emotional reaction from hearing the break.

Songs played are coded to help identify the station's music performance. Each is noted by title, artist, song classification, tempo (on a 1-4 scale with 4 being fastest), and era (80s, 90s, current). Your song coding will probably be different. Remember, this is just an example.

Station: WXYZ   **Talent Name**: Bob & The Breakfast Bunch

Date: 3/11/99   **Hour**: 7-8am   **Monitored by**: Tracy Johnson

Time	Element	Notes

7:01   Legal ID (Recorded)-tease news coming up-
introduce song
> Bob did the whole setup and intro with no interaction from the rest of Breakfast Bunch-smooth, but would like to get interaction from at least one of the other members of the "bunch".

"Fields of Gold"   Sting   Mainstream   2   90s

7:05   Live Break. Three phone calls on topic (set up in 6am hour). Quick Weather/Traffic and news headline used to tease news.
> Great break. It was quick, moved fast and transitioned well into the service elements. Phone calls were quick and Renea had a great punchline on the third call. Excellent job in resetting the topic going into the phone calls.

Station Promo: Music Image
7:09   Spot Break – 4 spots

7:13   Breakfast Bunch "rejoiner"…Bob & Renea tease "Battle of The Sexes" over song intro.
> Effective break. They were specific with the tease to make me want to listen, but forgot to tell me exactly when "Battle" would begin. Didn't mention prizes up for grabs,

but that's not as important as the contest itself. Sounded like they couldn't WAIT for it to begin!

"If You Leave"	**OMD**	**Alternative/Pop**	**3**	**80s**

7:17   Backsell song/promoted "at-work listening" and midday personality
        Excellent-tight and concise…used OMD song to demonstrate type of music to expect coming up at 9-really tied show to the rest of station.

7:18   Traffic/Weather/News
        News stories were too long. Need to edit the content and get to more stories. Also remind them to choose stories that interest the listener, not the ones that happen to be on the front page of the paper. The new formatics of putting traffic and weather before news sounds great, but they're not comfortable with it yet. Need to work on the mechanics! Probably a better "blackout" line would help.

7:21   Spot Break-4 spots

7:25   Quick phoner with Battle of Sexes Contestants challenging each other and talking trash — introduce song
        Great! Used listeners (both quite good) to sell the same element effectively! Both contestants were uptempo and played their role quite well (were they live or recorded?). Be sure to credit the producer! However, should have played the station rejoiner coming out of spots…missed an opportunity.

"Slide"	**Goo Dolls**	**Mainstream**	**4**	**Cur.**

Summary:
        Average Music Tempo: 4
        Current: 33%   Recurrent: 0%   90s: 33%   80s: 33%

        Show was uptempo, consistent and well promoted. Did a great job focusing on the basics and complementing each other. Work on sounding more spontaneous with each other and bringing out personality in the more "mundane" parts of the show!

MINUTE BY MINUTE MONITOR

It's usually not a good idea to compare any station or show directly with a competitor. However, there are many reasons to stay abreast of other stations and use a comparison tactic to help evaluate your performance.

One of the most effective ways to check up on who is winning the most important images ("top of mind," "service," "topicality," etc.) is a Minute by Minute Competitive Monitor.

It's easy to do, and will help you spot areas that may need improvement. Simply track everything that happens on two (or more) stations every single minute of an hour. Here's an example:

Station A	Time	Station B
Song: Nothing Compares	7:01a	Phone poll: Sex in public places
Song: Nothing Compares	7:02a	Phone poll: Sex in public places
Song: Nothing Compares	7:03a	Traffic/Weather
Talk about upcoming concerts	7:04a	Spot: Grocery Barn
Listen to win tickets & backstage	7:05a	Spot: Phil's Gas Station
Talk about TV show last night	7:06a	Spot: ABC TV Network
Spot: Downtown night club	7:07a	Station promo: Music Hooks
Spot: Ace Furniture	7:08a	Song: Runaround
Spot: 5th Street Records	7:09a	Song: Runaround
Spot: Friskies Cat Food	7:10a	Song: Runaround
Tease "Battle of Sexes"	7:11a	Talkover song intro/tease news
Song: All I Wanna Do	7:12a	Song: Hand In My Pocket

You get the idea...track every single minute and fill out the form in detail with information about what is talked about and each topic. Be sure to include detail about promos (what hooks were used, positioning on station and show, etc.).

Use this exercise monthly for each primary competitor and you'll be more alert to hitting the hot topics first!

SECTION

5

OTHER ASPECTS

CHAPTER

14

USING
THE
TELEPHONE

The telephone is a personality's best friend. Always remember that when it is ringing constantly, and it seems that every call is a little kid wanting to hear the latest hit from the current teen sensation. Used properly, the telephone provides a never-ending supply of information, entertainment, and material for the show.

Used improperly, the phone will derail a show. The person on the phone represents every listener. The talent that makes a caller uncomfortable or appear foolish makes all listeners feel that way. So treat listeners with care.

Too many personalities think of the telephone as an annoyance or intrusion. But these are real listeners who care enough about the show to want to talk to the talent! It's fine to pick up the phone and just ask them to hold for a second, but it's not okay to let it go unanswered. Don't ignore your customers!

There is magic to using the phone properly, and it takes time and experience to master the art of handling listener calls.

TREAT CALLERS WITH RESPECT

Each caller represents the total audience. Think about that. They are in control of every talent's ultimate destiny. It's not the employer that pays wages. It's the listener. The employer only handles the money. Talking down to a caller is talking down to the entire audience. When that is taken into account, most personalities react differently to the telephone. The studio is hectic. It's easy to ignore or "blow off" the phones. But to the caller, you are one of the most important people in their life.

Treat callers with respect. Thank them for calling (on or off the air), take an interest in them. Praise them. Tell them how glad you are they called. Make them feel good about participating and they'll feel good about "voting" for their favorite personalities!

> **Talent Tip:**
> Put a listener in a position to feel like a valid contributor, and they'll feel like a "star."

Another great tactic is to award random prizes to callers on the air. It helps get rid of the prizes that need to be distributed and encourages more calls. Plus, listeners who are given a prize for "no reason" will tell their friends about their positive experience with the radio. Radio stations win listeners one at a time, and lose them the same way!

> **Talent Tip:**
> The average customer who has been pleased by a company tells three people about it. The average customer who has had a problem with a company tells ten people about it. *

TREAT LISTENERS LIKE CUSTOMERS!

When's the last time you had a bad experience with a waitress, salesperson, or other customer service representative? How did it make you feel about that business? Maybe you gave them "one more chance" to earn or keep your business, but if they let you down again, they probably lost your support forever.

In radio, we are in the public relations business, and the person assigned to answer the telephone is on the "front lines" of customer service. When listeners call your show their experience is the most direct and intimate impression they have in forming opinions on the personality, the station, and the company. That's heavy responsibility,

> **Talent Tip:**
> Don't lose customers. Getting a new customer takes at least 50% more effort than gaining the same amount of listening from an established listener. *

and broadcasters usually don't take it as seriously as they should.

With all that happens to make a radio station sizzle, the customer that takes the time to call is usually a low priority, often the last consideration. But they are one of the most important. Imagine calling a restaurant for a reservation, and having the phone go unanswered. Or calling for half an hour only to receive a busy signal? Then, when you do get through, the receptionist is rude, impatient and obviously can't wait to get you off the phone so they can get back to something more important!

That's the experience too many people have when they call radio stations. These are people who take the time to participate actively in your business, and deserve to be treated like the valuable customers they are.

If listeners take the time to call you, the least you can do is spend a few seconds talking to them. You win listeners one at a time, but you lose them a dozen at a time if you are rude. If Mark McGwire signs his autograph for hours at a time, you can be nice to listeners. Remember, you're always performing, always creating impressions.

Whoever is assigned the duty of interfacing with listeners on the phone needs to be trained to handle all listener calls courteously and quickly, and contribute to the caller having a positive experience with the station.

Talent Tip:
Rule #1: The listener is always right.
Rule #2: If the listener is ever wrong, reread Rule #1.

After all, if the clientele is not treated well at the restaurant, it doesn't matter how good the food is. You won't go there!

MAKE THEM FEEL LIKE STARS! AND THEY'LL MAKE YOU A STAR!

The best way to get listeners to provide material and contribute regularly is to make them feel valuable. There's an art to making phone calls part of the entertainment of a show, and an effective method is reflecting the spotlight back on the caller. Air personalities who master that art will never have to worry about great, airable phone calls because listeners will jam the lines to talk with them.

It starts with a humble, "approachable" attitude and presentation. Make them feel like you are their "friend," someone non-threatening. Mark Jagger of Star 100.7 in San Diego is a master at welcoming listeners to the show. When a listener calls with a compliment for him or the station, Mark accepts it, and immediately reflects the attention back on the caller. He then directs the conversation where he wants it to go, but makes the listener feel like a million bucks for calling.

A typical example is in the following exchange:

> **Caller:** Hi! I just called to tell you that your station and your show is the best thing that happens to me. I couldn't get through a day without you.
>
> **Personality:** Oh my gosh…you made my day. What is it about your day that makes it so challenging?
>
> **Caller:** I'm a receptionist and I have to deal with the public all day long, and they really get to me sometimes…and it's just good to hear how much fun you guys are.
>
> **Personality:** Tell me…what's the most difficult caller you've had to deal with this week.
>
> **Caller:** Tells the story.
>
> **Personality:** Well, thank you for calling…you hang in there, and if there's ever anything I can do for you, you call back, okay?

Notice how the personality takes something generic (an "I love your show" call) and makes it:

1. Entertaining, through the story the listener tells
2. Personal and relatable, by treating the caller like a valuable person
3. Gets them to compliment the show and station TWICE

Practice the art of showcasing your callers by being inquisitive and asking questions of others. Be interested and listen to what others have to say in your every day life.

Quality Of Calls

One of the biggest problems personalities face is finding a phone call that adds to the show. We've found that the best way to get great phone calls is to air great phone calls. It's like the time you were looking for that first job in radio and were told to "get some experience and come back," right? It is a dilemma. Listeners want to contribute to a radio show, but they need to know it's "safe" to call and that they're not going to waste their time.

Each time a good call is aired, you send a message to your listener that the air talent is approachable, and they might actually get to talk to the "star."

Not only that, they might get on the air and contribute (humor, enthusiasm, controversy, etc) something to the broadcast, and actually be a part of the show. They can be a STAR.

In a way, you're training your listeners to participate. You will reap what you sow. Put on BAD calls, and you'll get more BAD calls. Boring people will respond to boring phone calls. So the best way to generate great content from your listeners is to be selective in what you accept on the air.

Some days, it's just impossible to find a great call. That's when your "ringers" become valuable. Keep a list of active, willing participants who are ready to contribute any time they're needed, and use them liberally. Good producers keep a list of people they can count on to provide a great sound bite at any time.

> **Talent Tip:**
> **Weak callers are best treated like under-performing stocks. Get rid of them, and move on to something that can be a winner for you.**

GETTING CALLS

So, if great calls bring more calls, how can you get the ball rolling? How can listeners be encouraged to call, especially on a new show? It's not as simple as just saying, "Call now and talk to us." What if the phones just don't ring? Sometimes they don't, and new shows often mistake that for a lack of appeal. That's not always the case. Usually, listeners just haven't been conditioned to respond yet. When you need phone calls, construct your material to improve your chances at creating listener responses.

Passion Drives Phones: The more passionate the talent is, the better the response will be. It's also more entertaining. Talk about things that are relevant to the talent and the audience. Talk without passion is chatter. Chatter is boring. Boring is a tune-out. Take a position, build some drama, state your opinion, and let the listeners take over.

Hot Current Events Drive Phones: Avoid generic topics that aren't relatable (gun control, abortion, etc.) to a person's normal, every-day life. The hotter the topic, the more controversial, the better. It has to be personal to be emotional, and it has to be emotional to be memorable.

Promos Drive Phones: Train listeners how to respond through strategic promos that demonstrate how they should react. Need phones? Put promos on that demonstrate callers as the showcase. It sends a message that "it's okay to call."

Polls Drive Phones: Listeners love to feel like they make a difference and their opinion counts. Seek their input, ask for information. Tell them you need their help, and don't be shy about it. Present it as, "Hey, we need your help with this," not "Now you have a chance to."

Themes Drive Phones: Continue the hot topic into the next hour, the next day, the next week! Play the hits! Just be sure to come up with a new angle and approach. If listeners know what to expect in a phone participation segment, they'll be ready to help out.

Set-Ups Drive Phones: Learn to lead listeners to contribute more. Don't give all of the argument. Leave out some facts, and let the listener contribute, filling in the gaps. Let them feel like they are the stars. Talk hosts call this the concept of "dummying up."

COACHING LISTENERS

The best source of phones is the request line, and a wealth of material awaits, but a lot of them need help. The producer (or phone screener) should constantly scan the phone lines to find enthusiastic listeners who match the target of the station. If you like the sound of a caller, ask them questions about the topic on the air right now:

1. Hey, what do you think about _____?
2. Has _____ ever happened to you?
3. Will you go on the air with us?

After screening the call, coach them to fit into the topic. Put words in their mouth. Okay, here's what I want you to say…get right to the point…and say it just like this. Then they'll take it from there. Got it?

If they're shy or uncomfortable, make them feel good about it. "Hey, you'll be great. Just be natural. The show really needs your help." If you can't get a paragraph from them, get a sentence. If you can't get a sentence, get a phrase. If you can't get a phrase, get a word! Milk the call to find something usable!

If you find a great caller, ask for their phone number and call them after the show. You should put together a list of "ringers" that you can call from time to time to get a bit going. They'll be flattered, and you'll have instant material anytime you need it. Plus, they'll start understanding what is expected of them and contribute on their own.

Similarly, contest winners (and participants) need coaching. They need to be enthusiastic and excited. The Price Is Right won't put a dull, bored contestant on the air. Neither should a radio show. There's nothing more deadly than a less-than-enthusiastic winner. And it's not their fault if the talent puts them on the air that way.

The phone screener has to prepare the contestant to go on, and make something useful and fun when it may not be that way naturally.

By the way, "stupid" listeners can be very useful. One of TV's most successful shows ever is "Wheel of Fortune." They deliberately select contestants judged to be slightly slower than the average at-home viewer, which guarantees that the viewer will "get it" before the contestant. It keeps viewers involved and makes them feel good (emotional response). Just don't be mean to listeners. Be polite to idiots, then make a comment that the audience can be "in on." Or, let them go and let your audience laugh at them. But you should not put yourself in a position of appearing mean-spirited.

Making a listener enthusiastic is not always easy, but they can be coaxed into it. Tell them they have to talk really loud to cut through on the air and be heard. This naturally brings up their enthusiasm if it's low.

PHONE CALL EXECUTION

If the talent gets the right call on the air, it's now up to them to make the call entertaining. The most important thing is to *stay in control* of the conversation. The talent directs the call, decides when it's over and moves on. The call needs to be steered to the desired goal, even if it makes the talent feel they are being rude to the caller.

Always avoid the "hi, who's this, where are you calling from" introduction. It's boring! Nobody cares! Get right into it. Know who is calling. "Hi Carol, what's up?" is enough. Remember, the audience hates long setups. Get right to it. Conduct the conversation with the "over the air" listener in mind.

When the payoff is hit, move on to the next element or next call. Don't say good-bye. Thank the caller OFF the air, or have the producer finish the call. The caller won't mind. They're excited that they have been on the air.

Always try to address each caller by name, and refer to it throughout the conversation in a natural, friendly way. Don't make fun of odd-sounding names. This will make all listeners feel more comfortable with the show, and encourage more participation.

Be quick to get a disappointing caller off the air. If it's not as entertaining as desired, move on! Sometimes it's possible to turn a weak call into something useful, but not often. Cut the losses and get on to something more entertaining.

Save That Call!

All, or at least most, phone calls should be recorded for future use. The talent will never be frustrated by having a great response giving you a great line but not be able to get it on the air. Phone calls can also be used out of context by strategically grabbing excerpts from previously recorded calls. Create an illusion of a listener always being there with a sharp comment. The more that illusion is created, the more likely they will make it a reality by calling in with great reactions.

Every day, someone should go through the phone log tape and edit it. Sometimes there'll be great calls that can be used in entirety with minor editing. Sometimes there'll be bits and pieces that can contribute in the future. Even a simple "Hi, how ya doing" will make a great drop for the show. Remember, phone calls (even in short-form) produce more phone calls. Train the audience to contribute.

Keep all the good calls, and log the content so it's easy to find. Be sure to edit them to make them fast-paced and tight. Use the good stuff, dump what isn't.

CHAPTER

15

PRODUCERS

*Not everyone can be a hero. Someone has to sit on the
curb and clap as the hero marches past.*

Too often, stations spend big bucks on the talent and forget about the supporting cast. A good producer can be the difference between a profitable investment in talent and a disaster. In fact, many high profile morning shows now have an assistant producer, or two!

If your producer is the guy who makes sure the coffee is hot and the doughnuts are fresh, you don't have a producer…you have a "gofer"!

Since consistency is the key to establishing a show, it's important that the producer be versatile, flexible, and able to work with (and sometimes around) the talent to achieve smooth consistency and day-to-day flow.

Most personalities know they need a producer, but really don't know what they are looking for, or how to evaluate what they have. They tend to find someone who makes them feel good, which is important, but not as important as someone who makes them *sound* good.

A producer's role will vary from show to show. The perfect "fit" is someone who provides direction, leadership, and a set of skills that complement those of the personality. If a show is set up properly, and understands the role of the talent on the air, the traits that are needed will be quite apparent and a search for the right producer will be much easier.

WHAT, OR WHO, IS A PRODUCER?

At the very least, a producer keeps everything updated in the studio. At best, he or she should be able to really "drive" the show.

> **Talent Tip:**
> **A great producer is an asset to the talent AND the PD. He or she acts as an on-field coach…the PD of the show!**

In many cases, the producer serves as a surrogate program director, while keeping the talent organized, on schedule, and fulfilling the mission statement developed in the planning sessions. That suggests that a good producer must be able to balance the personality and creativity of the morning talent and the formatic, strategic interests of the PD. That's sometimes a delicate balance and difficult to navigate.

Knowing the talent and having their respect is vital. Without it, a producer will be ineffective. The talent, and the programmer, must trust the producer.

Most producers handle all the details and help relieve the talent of the burden of having to think about anything except entertaining the audience.

Great producers have a keen sense of what is going on now, not just in the community and in the world, but in the studio, at any moment. Producers know what is important to the listener, and figure out how to help the talent present their material in an entertaining manner. Producers always should have a sense of having one ball in the air.

> **Talent Tip:**
> **Talent must trust the producer implicitly. The PD must trust the producer implicitly. The person who can gain the trust of both parties is rare!**

On a bad or slow day, they are a cheerleader, helping bring the mood of the studio up and making the talent forget about any distractions. The next day may require a completely different approach.

In the show structure, there is no room for a producer with an ego. This is a role of a servant, willing to take a back seat and let the talent be the star. Their sense of accomplishment comes when the talent receives recognition. They must be have a strong sense of themselves and take pride in how great they can make their talent.

Some producers double up with production or voice-work, increasing their value to the station even more. In fact, a carefully selected producer should not only help a show sound better, but be a training program for future APD or programming assistant positions.

BASIC SKILLS REQUIRED OF A PRODUCER

There are some things that are "nice to haves" in a producer. Many skills that make a show work are arbitrary and some shortcomings can be overcome by distributing responsibilities among other show members.

There are other elements that are "must-haves" if the producer is to help the talent reach its potential. Organization is the most basic element. Producers always have a lot of balls in the air at one time. Answering to the PD, working with promotions, dealing with sales, screening phone calls, keeping track of the flow of the show, directing the talent requires that the producer be able to multi-task and keep track of every little detail.

Execution is also central to effectiveness. Once the show is organized, it has to be put together in a smooth, well-planned (and seemingly spontaneous) show. The producer has to follow through and be flexible enough to react to unplanned situations without losing sight of the end result. Seizing the moment, and understanding what works, is crucial.

The producer must also act as the show's "editor." Face it, talent thinks that the more they talk, the better the show. It's the producer's job to keep them moving. The editor directs the talent to keep the elements at a manageable level. Usually, less is more, and it's the producer's job to make sure that less is achieved.

The producer must also be creative, especially in taking ideas to the air. He or she also must exercise judgement on what will and won't work with the talent.

All producers should be able to offer at least the following:

Strategic Focus

A producer must understand the station, the goals of the program director and how the talent fits into the structure. He or she must know what is expected and maintain a big picture focus that keeps the talent on track.

Further, the producer must have an intimate understanding of the show. They must know the role of each member of the cast, and how they fit into the show. The producer must direct each member to stay within their role and stay on track.

Structure

If there is to be any communication and preparation between the characters on the show, the producer should expect to be responsible to make it happen. The talent rarely has the discipline to meet weekly, let alone daily. It's the producer that has to make it happen. The producer is responsible for organization and show prep assignments.

He or she also must know what's going on at the station to keep the talent updated on what needs to be promoted. A lot of the producer's job is to attend meetings and facilitate communication. It's essential to the synchronicity of the show and the station.

Content

In addition to organizing all the show prep, the producer should be the one who comes up with stories and turns them into ideas for bits or promotions. He or she should also keep a detailed calendar of events and database of information for daily reference.

Audio Files

If the show doesn't have a "librarian," it's the producer's job to make sure everything is cataloged and filed for future use. Keeping an efficient, useful library will make the show sound spontaneous and in touch when something happens. Include data files, audio (sound effects, TV and movie drops, music beds, parody songs, production elements, etc.). You never know when you'll need to grab a drop from "Caddyshack" to accent a bit. The producer needs to organize a system that makes it possible to access it on a moment's notice.

Contacts

One of the most valuable tools a show can have is a list of important people and experts that can be interviewed at a moment's notice. A great producer never throws away a phone number, and works constantly to update the rolodex with new contacts. This list includes celebrities, past

Talent Tip:
Try to remember all names and faces...not just the important ones. You never know when someone will become valuable.

guests, and individuals who can help the show in any way.

The producer also is responsible for media contacts, locally and nationally. Establishing relationships with newspapers, magazines, online content providers, and trade publications will be invaluable when you need a "favor." The producer is the liaison between the show and media.

Networking

Establish relationships with other shows and producers to network with. When someone comes up with a great idea, or parody song, trade that information. It can make you look (and sound) like a hero!

Technical Skills

The ability to edit audio, run the board, screen phone calls, and set up equipment is not difficult to learn, especially in the digital age. It's also a fundamental that all producers need to master. Technical skills and production capabilities are a must.

The ability to screen phone calls and "set up listeners" is an art that can be learned. The producer that can coax callers into contributing to the show with a punchline, properly worded question, or conditioned response can make a huge difference.

Writing

The producer should be able to write creative promos or generate ideas that showcase the image and concept of the show. This is another example of the need to be philosophically aligned with the PD, to keep those promos in synch with the station's goals. Along with the proper production expertise, the producer should be able to supervise the promo project from beginning to end.

> **Talent Tip:**
> Demand the best performance from your producer. Remember, it's not the producer you replace that makes your life miserable. It's the ones you don't. Find the RIGHT one, and KEEP them.

Producer Tasks

Some of the traits to look for in a producer:

1. Organizational Skills
   - Detailed notes on each day's show
   - Keep the talent on-time and following schedule
   - Finalize daily prep sheets
   - Maintain weekly planner
   - Maintain show files for future reference
   - Arrange guests
   - Coordinate appearances with promotion/programming
   - Librarian for bits, production, "best of" archives, etc.
   - Answer listener questions, send out correspondence

2. Show "Director"
   - Make the talent look good
   - Keep talent on the game plan during and after the show
   - Offer input into the show and keep talent moving forward
   - Regroup the players when it's just not "working"
   - Be a cheerleader

3. Production
   - Edit tape, record phone bits, etc.
   - Run the studio
   - Produce beds, best of shows, edit & prepare show prep

SECTION

6

HIRING A SHOW

CHAPTER

16

How
To
Hire
A
Show

When it comes to hiring or building a morning show, most stations start looking for what Alan Burns calls the "silver bullet," a pre-existing morning team that: a) is very successful in their market, b) knocks your socks off in a three minute tape, c) is not under contract, and d) is not very

> **Talent Tip:**
> **When hiring a new show, look in unusual places. It's often easier to teach entertaining people how to do great radio than train radio people how to be entertaining.**

expensive. Don't waste your time. You might as well hope for the FCC to revoke the license of all your major competitors.

More than likely, you'll have to do one or more of the following:

• If you find the right talent, wait for them to become available.

• Assemble your own show.

• Find a successful show, and spend several days listening to figure out why it works.

• Pay more than you think you should have to.

It's hard to find a morning show. There are few great ones, and even fewer available great ones. But there is nothing more important. If you are an aspiring morning talent looking for a station, there is nothing more important than being found.

In either case, knowing what you are looking for is the first step toward a successful partnership. Understand what is important and what isn't. Staying focused and relentlessly pursuing your dream show will pay off!

QUESTIONS FOR HIRING TALENT

Whenever a new talent is considered for a station, it's important to project how that show would sound on that station. How do they "fit" into the structure and personality of the station? Do you get along? Is there a good foundation for a working partnership?

When investigating a new show, watch carefully for subtle signs, and trust your instincts. Every veteran PD can tell you stories about mistakes they've made convincing themselves that the show would work, and "settling" on something that is less than ideal. You can't go strictly by "the book." There's more to this business than science. It's an art. It's a feel.

When you ask the typical questions, you'll get the typical responses. "Yes, I'm a team player. Yes, I take direction well. Yes, I work well with others. Yes, I believe that protecting the license is important."

Dig deeper in the hiring process. Talk in depth to all references, and try to get a "read" of your interviewee. Conduct multiple interviews with the candidates. Fly into their market unannounced to listen to a "typical" morning instead of relying on the air checks they have sent. Don't make snap judgements. Listen for several days. Try to understand the market so you can understand if the show is doing a good job fitting into it. Remember, great shows normally don't sound "great" to market outsiders on first listen. That's exactly what makes them great.

> **Talent Tip:**
> **When interviewing a new candidate, ask yourself how you'd feel if this person were working for your largest competitor rather than you.**

> **Talent Tip:**
> **Find talent that is ready to "fall in love" with a market, marry it, and begin a long-term relationship with listeners.**

Finally, ask open-ended questions. Then, shut up and listen. Let them talk. Look for consistent answers. Listen for honesty. Don't ask the standard interview questions. You want to measure their thought process, and how well they think on their feet. Look for intelligence. How well do they understand themselves? How well do they understand the business? How well do they understand their own success? If you're hiring an entire show, interview the members individually. Determine how well they understand their role in the show.

TALENT INTERVIEW QUESTIONNAIRE

There is no right or wrong answer to these questions. It is a place to start helping to determine if there is a good "match" between employer and talent. Also remember it's just a starting point. You can come up with dozens more.

1. What is your greatest success? What was the key to success? Who made it happen?

2. What is your biggest failure? What could have been done to prevent it? Who was responsible for it?

3. What do you like most in a boss or supervisor? What drives you nuts about them?

4. How do you feel about critiques? How often do you meet with management?

5. What would you do if a competing station taunted you or your family?

6. What job did you like best in your career and why?

7. If you were going on the air in a market and competing with yourself, what would you do to attract listeners away, and command market share?

8. What personalities do you most admire? Why?

9. What was your most successful promotion ever? What made it work? Would you do it again? How would it be better next time?

10. Is there a broadcasting company that you admire? Why?

11. What is the best bit you've done this month?

12. What is the best bit you've done this week?

13. What is the best bit you did today?

14. What is the worst bit you've done in the past month?

15. How do you prepare for your show?

16. Do you prefer live or taped phone bits?

17. How many songs per hour are right for your show? What's the most or least you are comfortable with?

18. What are the three best topics to have fun with right now? What have you done with them recently?

Next, ask the show to play a game with you. Call it the "Variety Game." Dave Robbins came up with this idea. Your goal is to find out how much they can extemporize about current events. It's very effective with a whole show, or with individuals.

In this exercise, you'll throw out some pre-selected topics and give them one minute to talk about each topic. After a minute, give them another topic. After four topics, reduce response time to 45 seconds, then 30, and then 15.

Make it rapid fire...cut them off at the end of each interval in mid-sentence. Make them shift gears in mid-stream. Topics should be customized to be current at the time of the interview and to fit the interests of your target audience. In other words, don't ask a morning show candidate for an 18-24 male station about social security.

Here's an example of 16 topics you could use:

Child Care	Education	Daycare
Movies	Baseball Salaries	Pornography
Rain Forests	Elections	AIDS
Success	John Travolta	Street Gangs
South Park	Domino's Pizza	Cheerleaders
Iraq		

This exercise gives you a great insight into a person's character. They will talk off the top of their head with little time to prepare or organize their thoughts. They won't be able to hide their attitudes, or their discomfort if they aren't informed about a topic.

It's also a great drill if you're building a new cast of personalities that have never worked together. You'll get to see how they react and interact spontaneously and under pressure.

> **Talent Tip:**
> *If you interview someone and don't immediately like him, don't hire him. The odds are that your instincts are right.*

AUDITIONING THE SHOW

Morning show auditions are an unnatural event for the performers and can be very difficult. They're in a strange studio, a strange city and under intense pressure to give you what they think you want.

Still, an on-air audition in the middle of the night can be a useful tool. Just be sure you know how to use it.

First, don't expect the show to be perfect. There will be mistakes, and they will be nervous. But, DO expect them to be prepared, informed, and ready to give you 100%, even if you haven't asked for it.

The PD should lay out basic direction, including who the target audience is. Then, put them in a studio for a couple of hours to get comfortable and prepare. Don't listen in, and don't let them see you.

During the audition, take detailed notes about everything. Notice how they handle phone calls, how they guide the listener through the call. How comfortable are they with each other? Are the roles well defined? How do they promote the station? Are they consistent with service elements? Write down everything. You'll want to refer to it later.

Following the on-air audition, give them some time to unwind. Later, critique their performance bluntly and honestly. Not so much to correct them, but to see how they react to your direction and input. Be direct. Explain how you want the show to sound and why.

Grill them about what they think the audience is interested in. What will be their preparation process for the next show? Did they learn anything from their audition? What is their angle? Their attitude and mood? Watch to see who takes the lead in the meeting, and how they conduct themselves. Do they have good judgment? Are they offended at your involvement? Scared?

Then, put them back on the next overnight to see how they alter the presentation (they'll also be more comfortable).

Meet again the following day and repeat the critique, break by break. Get their input this time. Listen to how they assess their performance. Self-evaluation in a show is critical.

Believe In The Show, Believe In Yourself

If you have a winning show, and believe in yourself and your future, don't let anyone talk you out of it! Keep searching for the PD and the company that shares your vision, supports your ideas, and gives you the creative license to fulfill our dreams.

Once there was a television executive who had a vision for a new sit-com built on family values, moral living, and making a positive difference in people's lives. The idea flew directly in the face of what was "working" in network television at the time. "What, you're going to ram your ethics and values down the throats of middle America in a sit-com? It'll never work," was the prevailing "wisdom" in corporate boardrooms.

The executive never gave up. He wouldn't listen to naysayers or be discouraged by those who told him that a TV show whose pilot taught family values about dealing with death through the passing of a goldfish was ridiculous. He pressed on, relentlessly seeking a network that would listen. He stuck to his idea and even mortgaged his future in dogged pursuit of his dream.

Finally, he found a backer, a network willing to gamble on his concept. A decade later, when "The Cosby Show" concluded its dominant run of success, Tom Warner was rewarded when critics praised his creation as one of the most unique, inspiring, and original ideas in the history of television.

CHAPTER

17

Tips For New Shows

You have only one chance to make a first impression.

Maybe your new show isn't on the air now. Maybe you'll search for months and not find the answer. All is not lost. In many cases, you're better off building your own show from scratch. If you do, follow the principles explained in the early sections of this book. And proceed slowly.

First, don't pre-promote a new show unless it's a well-known show that is widely loved by your listeners. A show that is returning to the market or moving across the street fits that description, but that's about all. New, unfamiliar morning shows — even those that become huge successes — rarely live up to the expectation if they are hyped in advance. It's a terrible way to start.

Whenever a new show is added to a station, first impressions are critical. It's second nature for a show to want to be promoted with a million-dollar ad campaign shortly after they debut. But it's not smart. Before a show is marketed, it must sound great. And before it can sound good, it must be comfortable. In fact, you shouldn't even promote a new show on your own air until they are "ready." It puts you at a disadvantage to build up expectations that can't be fulfilled.

Make sure a new show understands the format, the city, and the audience very well.

Don't try to do too much out of the box. Hit singles until you hit your stride. As you grow and develop, you can start swinging for the fences and eventually start hitting home runs. This is especially true if you have new cast members and are not familiar with the roles each person will fill.

Prioritize the elements in your show, and start slowly. Establish the basics first, and add the more entertaining elements around these principles. Remember, you have to MASTER the basics. Until you do, the rest doesn't matter. Here is a great checklist to start building a new show. How will you use these elements? What is the philosophy for each item, filtered through your mission statement? This checklist will help you further define who you are on the air, and by defining who you are, you will find it easier to put all of these elements in the proper perspective.

1. **Service Elements**
   - Weather/temperature checks
   - Time checks
   - Traffic
2. **News**
   - Local Stories
   - National Stories
   - Human Interest
   - Sports
3. **Information**
   - Lifestyle bits aimed at your audience
   - Music
   - Movies/TV/Entertainment info
   - Celebrity gossip/Tabloid trash
4. **Localization**
   - Local news events/coverage
   - Public Service involvement
   - Local characters
   - Local celebrities
   - Local sites
5. **Humor**
   - Humorous discussion of national and local stories
   - Comedy drops from albums, TV, and movies
   - Parody songs
   - Pre-recorded parody commercials, etc.
6. **Listener Involvement**
   - Listeners MUST be the star
   - Phone polls
   - Listener participation
7. **Stunts**
   - Challenge the listener
   - Attention-getting stunts by the morning show

8. Fun & Games
- Trivia
- Contesting
- Listener participation bits

9. Remotes
- Look for reasons to celebrate important dates, especially local
- "Meet every listener" campaign
- How often will we be on the streets?

10. Guests
- Unusual, provocative guests
- Authors always want to be on the air. Will they be on your show?
- Celebrity interviews? How, when, and why?

11. Good Guys
- How involved will you be in the community?
- How will you make your show "endearing?"

12. Major Promotions
- Will all major station promotions be driven by the morning show?
- Will there be a major morning show promotion supported by the station?

13. Production
- Jingles
- Music
- Parodies
- Listener drops

When debuting a new show, it's a good idea to have some rehearsals before the official debut. Start in a production studio for a few days, then graduate to overnights for about a week. Get comfortable with the studio, the equipment, and how everything will work. It eliminates a lot of future problems.

BUILDING A MORNING SHOW CLOCK

Building a formatic clock for a new show is really very simple. Just like building a house, always start with the foundation, the elements that never change from hour to hour. First, put in positions for stop sets. Then add in music, news, traffic, weather, etc.

Then, add in the entertainment elements, leaving room to pre-sell any specific upcoming bits.

When developing your clock, remember that morning listeners are transient. So, consider each hour to be a series of three 20-minute shows. Each 20-minute period should represent a snapshot of what you, your show, and your station are all about. Each segment should contain all of the key elements you want to give your listener. Information, service elements, music, humor, promotion, benchmarks, etc. Then, every 20 minutes, start it all over again!

This obviously means you have to repeat information you really want your audience to "hear." Repeat bits, recycle material, and be bold in giving your audience the "hits" of the day!

Of course, your show may take a detour from your map, and each hour may take a different direction, but you should stay on track unless there is a good reason to deviate.

There are many ways to display the hour, the most popular being the graphical (circular) clock and the linear clock. I've always preferred the linear clock, because it allows you to be more detailed and show all of the formatics in an hour. It's also easy to alter for any specific hour. For example, you could write in the title of each song in the hour.

You may prefer the circular because it's easier to read and you get a quick "snapshot" of where you are in the hour. Examples of each are included.

For all new shows especially, start with the basics and add more complex elements as the show develops.

Here are two sample clocks to get you started. You'll want to create a form to build your own.

CLOCK 1 ASSUMES: 8 songs per hour

4 traffic reports

2 newscasts per hour

12 spots (4 stops/3 units ea)

CLOCK 2 ASSUMES: 6 songs per hour

3 traffic reports

1 newscast per hour

16 spots (4 stops/4 units ea)

Day/Date _____**Hour**_____

:00   Legal ID — recorded element
     Song #1   Power Gold _____

:04   Back-sell Song. Pre-sell upcoming feature
     _____ (open break for 2:00 content)

:07   Commercials 3:00
     Traffic/Weather out of stop set
     Cue: "I'm (name) with (show name) on WXYZ"

:12   Recorded "rejoiner" element
     Song #2   Recurrent _____

:15   Talkover Intro of song-quick phone call if it fits
     Song #3   Power Current _____

:19   Back Sell Song
     _____ (open break for 2:00 content)

:21   News 1:00   Jock Intros, QUICK banter going into News
     Traffic/Weather
     Cue: "I'm (name). More (show name) next on WXYZ"

:22   Commercials 3:00
     Pre-sell upcoming feature

:25   Introduce song
     Song #4   Power Gold _____

:29   Talkover Intro of song-quick phone call if it fits
     Song #5   Secondary Current _____

:33   Back Sell Song
     Hour's Best Feature _____ (3:00)

:36   Commercials 3:00
     Traffic/Weather out of stop set
     Cue: "I'm (name) with (show name) on WXYZ"
     Song #6   Power Recurrent _____

:43   Talkover Intro-quick phone call if it fits
       Song #7   Power Gold _____

:47   Back Sell Song/Pre Sell next hour
       _____(open break for 2:00 content)

:49   News Headlines (tease for next hour)
       Interactive break with show and news person

:51   Commercials 3:00
       Traffic/Weather out of stop set
       Jock intros traffic/Show does weather/intro song

:56   Song #8   Power Current _____

Promote This Hour: _____

Major Station Promotion: _____

Minor Station Promotion: _____

Best Bit This Morning: _____

Best Bit This Week: _____

Coming Up Next Week: _____

Day/Date _____ Hour_____

:00   Legal ID — Live over intro of song
        Song #1   Power Gold _____

:04   Back-sell Song. Pre-sell upcoming feature
        This hour's prime feature _____ #1
        _____ (open break for 4:00 content)

:08   Commercials 4:00

:12   Traffic/Weather out of stop set
        Cue: "I'm (name) with (show)…Now (song) is on WXYZ"
        Song #2   Recurrent _____

:17   Back Sell Song
        Shorter break-self contained
        _____ (open break for 2:00 content)

:19   Commercials 4:00

:23   News 2:00   Jock Intros, QUICK banter going into News
        Traffic/Weather
        Cue: "I'm (name) with (show). Now, (song) is on WXYZ
        Pre-sell upcoming feature
        Song #3   Power Current _____

:30   Talkover Intro of song-tease upcoming element
        Song #4   Power Gold _____

:33   Back Sell Song
        Hour's Best Feature _____ (4:00)

:36   Commercials 4:00

:40   Traffic/Weather out of stop set
        Cue: "I'm (name) with (show name) on WXYZ"
        Song #5   Power Recurrent _____

:45   Back Sell Song
        _____ (open break for 4:00 content)

:50   Commercials 4:00
       Pre-sell Next Hour out of spots

:55   Song #6   Power Current _____

Promote This Hour: _____

Major Station Promotion: _____

Minor Station Promotion: _____

Best Bit This Morning: _____

Best Bit This Week: _____

Coming Up Next Week: _____

BEFORE A NEW SHOW HITS THE AIR

Before a new show hits the air, they must know the community. Really understanding what makes it "tick" takes time, sometimes years. But knowledge helps establish relatables more quickly. Every morning show should be able to pass this "relatables" test by immediately naming one or two recognized "best" or "favorite" answers in each category. By the way, if a veteran morning show has trouble with this test, you have bigger problems than you think!

Teach Your Listeners Well

Promotion of the show isn't as important as promoting the personalities. And, furthermore, promoting the personalities is not as important as promoting the desired mood that the personalities project.

The act of promotion is a function of learning. Try to teach the audience, the target, how to respond to your station, your personalities. So, if your mission is to teach the audience how to respond to your images, you must understand the learning process.

A basic principle of learning is that people can't really learn more than one thing at a time in any particular category. If you try to teach too many things, all elements will be confused, the respondent shuts down, and nothing is retained. Never try to create multiple images simultaneously. It'll seriously delay progress.

As the hierarchy of images you want to teach listeners develops, remember the FIRST image is most important. It's like constructing a pyramid. The biggest part goes on the bottom. So, if your mission statement is based on being a funny morning show, demonstrate humor exclusively until the audience "gets" it. Once that has been learned, you can put this trait in maintenance mode and develop another angle, such as "the show that has a soft heart for kids." But, if you try to do both at the same time, you'll never establish either.

MUSINGS

A Collection Of Short Subjects

There is so much more that morning shows and programmers need to know to maximize success. The following pages are a collection of ideas and thoughts that don't fit anywhere else in this book!

LEADERSHIP

Successful, highly paid air personalities have more responsibility than just being great while on the air. They also must be leaders. The rest of the staff will always take their "cue" from the biggest personalities.

Part of that responsibility is accepting a leadership role. Promoting the station, supporting other talent, executing formatics important to the overall success of the station. The more the station succeeds, the more successful the talent becomes, and vice-versa. If a talent is tired of the music, or bored with it, so what? The show is for the listener! It's their responsibility to sell it, whether they agree with it or not.

It's also important to be a role model for other employees. Attendance at important meetings, station functions and events sends a message to everyone that they are team players and care about more than themselves. Imagine an NFL quarterback deciding they don't need to attend the Monday morning meetings to review film or prepare with the rest of the team for next week's game!

Make your co-workers feel good about promoting you and supporting the show. You will strengthen your own performance when you establish a rapport with other employees. The old adage is true: The station that wins in the halls, will win on the air.

Great talent requires great radio stations to succeed. And vice versa. It's everyone's responsibility to do all they can to ensure success.

PROMOTING TEAMWORK

Basketball coach Rick Pitino meets with every member of the team individually and sets specific goals to meet that person's ultimate objectives. He doesn't treat everyone the same way. But each has a role in raising the performance of the team.

After establishing the goals of the individual, the next step is to raise the bar high. Set the goals for the entire team and tie them into individual goals. Then, provide feedback toward achieving those goals. Use quantitative and qualitative data in evaluation, and look for steady, regular improvement. Stations improve in stages, and as the level of performance increases, the standards by which individuals are measured rises. This leads to a genuine work ethic, which leads in turn to commitment to teammates, and ultimately, excellence.

10 ESSENTIALS TO PROVIDE TALENT

1. **Proper operating equipment.** The last thing you want them thinking about is if the studio equipment is going to work.

2. **The proper tools.** The cost of a prep service that a talent wants is usually minimal. Get as many as you can. If you're serious about talent, give them the support they need.

3. **Positive reinforcement.** Pile it on. Just like a kid, they can never hear good things often enough. Put it in writing, too.

4. **Make them feel special.** Give them perks, spiffs. Treat them like entertainers. Coddle them.

5. **Meet with them daily.** Let them know you listen and care about them.

6. **Make the show part of your game plan.** Get their feedback. When the station succeeds, let them know how instrumental they are in it.

7. **Show them the research.** Let them watch focus groups. Make them part of the process.

8. **Analyze successful shows in other markets.** Use them for brainstorming and ideas.

9. **Meet outside the station.** Let them have fun, take the pressure off.

10. **Pop into the studio occasionally,** especially when you hear a great segment.

MORE MUSIC MORNING SHOWS

Regardless of what research reports indicate, most stations won't win in the morning without a personality driven show. "More Music" morning shows are typically not very compelling, and finish behind the heavy hitters. The big winners (Bob & Tom, Howard Stern, Jeff & Jer) don't play any music at all!

The reason music in the morning usually doesn't work is that it can't gather any momentum. There's rarely a water cooler discussion about the DJ who introduces the new Alanis Morissette song. They want information, sports, and conversation to get going. Fulfilling the "most music" promise doesn't leave room for a lot of talk, and it takes time to make talk entertaining.

To the audience, their ideal hour would include 40 minutes of music, 40 minutes of fun and information. Plus, we have to play 12 minutes of spots, making it even more impossible. The personality shows take over, build momentum, and the listeners catch music later in the day.

Yes, we'd all like a fat-free Big Mac that was totally healthy and sacrifices no taste. But it won't work. To win, you have to understand what the audience reacts to, not merely what they say they want.

Still, there is a position in every market for a station that relies on music for it's key benefit in the morning. The key is to understand the dynamics that make it work.

Even though music is the "star," the show still must be unique, different, and "special." Morning radio usage is different from other dayparts, and morning shows must be different as well. Listeners need form and consistency in the morning. In addition to information elements (news, traffic, weather), create a concept in the morning. Have a different but reliable show each day with benchmarks to act as road signs that direct listeners through the show.

Just because music is the priority, personalities should still be interesting. In many ways, it's even more difficult to entertain while playing 10 songs an hour than it is playing four or five. Listeners are trying to wake up and get going, and even uptempo music will only stimulate them so far.

Make your listener think. Music features can achieve this, while supporting the position. Features can be entertaining, thought provoking and still allow for a lot of music.

Finally, be careful not to restrict the personality on the show to liners cards. Be real, human, and relatable. Make sure listener values and talking about what interests the audience reflects lifestyles.

LETTERMAN: THE PERSONALITY

If only he had been a radio personality. Maybe he still will make a career change and grace us all with the talent that belongs in our medium. David Letterman has the structure, fundamentals, and elements that make up the backbone of successful radio shows.

In typical Letterman style, here are the Top 10 reasons why Letterman would be America's finest radio personality:

#10. He's competitive. He's always looking for a way to keep the show entertaining and changing, while maintaining the basic structure of the program. The bits evolve, there are interesting twists, and he constantly reinvents himself.

#9. He recycles bits. Notice how Dave reuses film clips from previous shows or makes references to earlier programs. He is a master at tying bits together, turning small mundane elements into running gags. Story lines are developed through clever repetition.

#8. He takes shots at himself. The fun is at his own expense. He's not afraid to be the butt of the joke. Don't be afraid to laugh at yourself, and invite listeners to do the same.

#7. He keeps it simple. There's a monologue, the Top 10 list, interesting guests, and a musical segment. The show has an occasional "slice of life" video bit or stunt. There's nothing fancy. The framework is predictable, but the show is always fresh. Everybody "gets" the jokes, and can follow along.

#6. He's topical. He reads a lot, goes to the movies, watches TV and listens to the radio. He knows what's going on and is naturally curious. In other words, he's in touch with the world and the audience.

#5. He's true to himself. He knows who he is and what the appeal is, and stays within that personality. He has not compromised his material or the show to become more "mass appeal." He has developed a unique style and stuck to that formula for success.

#4. He's brief. Notice how quickly he rolls through the opening segment of the show. The Top 10 list never takes more than two or three minutes, but it's the highlight of the show! The gags are brief between guests and the show is fast-paced.

#3. He knows the audience. He knows what is timely and hip, and what isn't. He's not cutting edge, nor is he conservative. He's just far enough ahead of the curve to be refreshing.

#2. He's a team player. The band and regulars on the show are often spotlighted. He lets the guests and members of the audience be key contributors. Dave is in the spotlight, but he shines because he allows those around him to be stars.

#1. He's always prepared. Dave personally reviews every element of the show before it airs. He produces as well as performs. When Dave has chosen the Top 10 list, the writers come up with about 150 possibilities. They reduce it to the best 50, then take it to Dave for the final cut. A lot of effort goes into making the show sound spontaneous and effortless.

INTERVIEWS

Interviews can be a great entertainment vehicle, or they can be death. Most personalities include interviews at some point as a source to create audience response. There are some fundamental principles to follow when considering interviews.

Johnny Carson was a master of the interview for three reasons:

- He knew what his guest was all about (preparation). He did his homework.

• He made the interviewee comfortable. He got more out of them.

• He was a great facilitator. He drew people out with his comments.

Personalities who use interviews need to consider them events! Whether it's an entertainer, sports celebrity, or other notable personality, make each interview something listeners will remember, or don't bother.

The goal is to entertain the listener and find something they will want to tell others about. Ask questions listeners really want to know. Don't just talk about where the artist has been recently. Ask what is the worst place they have performed. Ask them to tell you something about themselves that would surprise us, something they've never told anyone before. Ask about secret passions and fears. What would they be doing if they weren't doing this?

When Howard Stern interviewed Maury Povich, he asked "Does Connie make more money than you?" and "Who have you had over for dinner lately?"

If you can't find the right questions, get help! Solicit input from other perspectives. Ask friends, station employees, and even listeners to contribute questions. Put listeners on the air to ask some sensitive questions.

Personalize the interviews, and include local references if possible. Ask if they've been to dinner in your town, and what their favorite things are about your city. Make suggestions on the air of where they should go, and what they should do. Humanize and localize the stars.

Be a great listener. Don't think about what you are going to say next. Listen intently and allow yourself to be spontaneous. You'll be amazed at how much smoother the conversation goes.

Finally, prepare! See the movie, read the book, know the music. Whatever the topic or interview, know what you are talking about.

NAMING A SHOW

A source of conflict between management and talent can often be what to name a show when it first hits the air. A good case can be made for giving the show a "generic" name, especially in smaller markets. A name like "The Morning Zoo" or "Breakfast Club" can soften the blow a station receives if and when one of the key members departs for a bigger opportunity. It may cause the talent's ego a setback, but promoted effectively, and handled correctly, the talent doesn't have to sacrifice any "star value" derived from their name.

On the other hand, be careful to stay clear of any preconceived notions or "sacred cows."

One concern is that the show's name often becomes a substitute for the name of the station. The Arbitron gods frown on this.

You should also take care to pick a name that has strategic or tactical application to the station. It's part of the "synchronization" of the show and the post-10am programming. Simply naming a show "Breakfast Club" may have value on certain levels. After all, you have to name the show something, and breakfast does describe the general time of day people will be listening, but it really contributes nothing to the strategic positioning of the show or station.

Ries & Trout say, "positioning is not what you do as a product. Positioning is what you do in the mind of the prospect." The art of position is not to create something new and different, but to manipulate what is already there in the mind and re-tie the connections that already exist. There are few listeners who consider a station the best station to "eat breakfast to." Since you can't create a position from a perception that doesn't exist, the handle "Breakfast Show" probably is ineffective.

"Morning Zoo," "Morning Madhouse," "Nut Hut" all have positioning value in that they relate a message that carries image about the type of show the listener can expect.

When choosing a name, remember that everything on the air pushes the listener away from the station or brings them closer. Everything. There is no neutral. The environment of morning radio is hectic, confusing, and rushed. The messages received by the listener are selective. If the message isn't relevant to them, the information is rejected.

In the continuing effort to create Arbitron recall, remove all meaningless, irrelevant messages that create clutter. This clutter causes real or perceptual tuneout. If the show's core name doesn't say something about the show or the station, it's part of the problem.

So, when naming the show, take your time. Brainstorm. Kick around fresh ideas. New, innovative concepts may seem strange at first, but with the proper positioning and branding, you can make it work, and add strategic value to you product.

How To Tell If You're Doing It Wrong

Most problem jocks have come from one of two things: Trying too hard, or an overblown ego.

You can tell you're not doing well on the air if:

- An acquaintance in another line of work asks you to say something in your "radio voice."
- You meet a listener who says you sound a lot different in person than you do on the air.
- You always emphasize the little words like "and," "the," "is," etc.
- You sound like you're reading to someone…especially if you sound like you're reading to children.
- You beg pardon every time you stumble on a word or phrase, and correct yourself with "excuse me," … "that should be," etc.

GAINING CREDIBILITY

In many ways, we tell our listeners what we think of them. They can sense it when we think of them as a large mass of audience, used to provide an object for our own brilliance.

They also sense it when we act in a caring way, concentrating on THEIR needs and wants. If you want your listener to LIKE you instead of merely tolerating you, here are some tips that can help.

1. **Respect their intelligence.** Avoid using big words, flaunting your intelligence, when smaller words will work. Don't show off, don't patronize, and assume that your listener is as smart as you are — but they may not be paying as much attention.

2. **Deliver on your promises.** Don't promote a giveaway "coming up," then, not run it. Be responsible. Don't assume that nobody will notice if you drop the record that you promised is coming up. It's probably somebody's favorite song. If you absolutely can't deliver on a promise, apologize for it and explain how you will make it up.

3. **Be unpredictable.** Step out of your radio persona. Be a real person.

4. **Show enthusiasm when talking to listeners both on and off air.** Listeners form an impression of you based on how you treat callers on the air.

5. **Stay fresh.** It's like a marriage that starts out with a lot of sparks only to have the newness wear off and become monotonous. You have to work on new material, new devices, and new angles to entertain your audience. Otherwise, they become bored.

6. **NO inside jokes or jargon.** Listeners don't know what a cart machine is. Also, every time you refer to something that has gone on before, such as a running gag, explain it to your listener as though it were the first time they heard it. It doesn't have to be long and involved, just enough to set the stage.

To relate and be one-to-one with your audience, you have to take care of them and put THEM first...not yourself.

TIPS FOR GREAT SHOWS

There are many ways to reflect listener tastes on the air. Keeping these insights in mind, here are some ideas you can use to improve your show:

- **RECYCLE:** Everything old can become new again. Great ideas are just ideas. Rework bits from years ago with a fresh twist.

- **TRY SOMETHING NEW:** Experiment. Be fresh everyday. At the same time, be consistent and dependable. There are thousands of ways to give away prizes. Don't just settle for "10th caller wins!" Take something consistent and mundane and make it fresh and new. Use listeners as part of the entertainment. And don't throw up your hands in disgust because the promotions department (or sales staff) gives you weak prizes. Find a way to make it interesting.

- **WHAT'S IN THE NEWS?** Be balanced. Some topics are funny, some are serious. A good show can handle both and be true to the show's overall mission statement. The important thing is to know how to touch people emotionally about what they care about.

- **INSIDE JOKES:** Being excluded from a conversation is uncomfortable. Don't do that to your listener! Never assume they know what you are talking about. Set it up again and re-state your topics and positions. This becomes a big issue as the show grows and develops a core group of listeners.

- **BASICS:** Execute the basics. Sell your position and the station. This is the foundation of the show!

- **CHARACTERS:** If they are a part of your show, consider their value and know how they fit the show. Keep the characters fresh. Replace the ones that are worn out with new ones.

- **TALK CHECK:** Don't fall into the trap of entertaining yourself or your guest at the expense of the listener. Be honest and objective in evaluating whether you are "on the mark." Be sure the show is truly fun to hear for the listener.

- **TIMING:** Attention spans are getting shorter and shorter. Set up bits quickly, get into it, and get into something else. Hit the peak and move on!

- **PREPARATION:** Set aside time to plan tomorrow's show.

- **MUSIC:** Be consistent. Agree in advance how much and what type…then DO it. EVERY day, EVERY hour. No exceptions. Consistency!

- **SPORTS:** Keep it simple, non-technical, and easy to understand, if at all. Many stations only use sports if they are an "event" or they look for the mass appeal aspects of sports.

- **TEASE IT:** Pre-promote everything. Keep people interested in what's going on. Tell them what you've done, and what you're going to do.

- **ARRIVE EARLY:** Update your Daily Road Map. Check the overnight news. Watch taped highlights of last night's TV. Be alert when you hit the air. Many shows don't "wake up" until 7:30, and by then they've missed a lot of opportunity.

THROW DOWN THOSE CRUTCHES!

If you are an air personality, especially a morning talent, be careful not to create excuses for failure. It's okay to fail. In fact, risking failure is essential or you'll never attempt anything important. It's *not* okay to set yourself up with excuses that may not have anything to do with success or failure, and which actually increase the odds that you *will* fail.

There are three emotional crutches that many talents use as reasons (excuses) why they aren't (or "can't") succeed:

- "I'd be more successful if the music were better." There may be some legitimate concerns about the music, or there may not. Tell the PD what you think, then forget about it. It's out of your control. Focus on things that *can* be controlled — your performance.

- "I'd be more successful if they'd promote me more." Probably not. External advertising of morning shows doesn't make them more entertaining. It does increase momentum for a show that's already heating up, or, in the case of a contest like the "Birthday Game," it may increase the cume for a short time. Talent gets people to listen by being consistently excellent. People talk about talent that creates entertainment, and word of mouth is the most valuable form of advertising.

- "I'd work harder if they paid me more." This is a tragic state of mind, and talent won't be successful until they overcome it. People who think this way have reversed cause and effect. In real life, you bust your butt, become a success and then you get paid commensurate with success.